STUDENT UNIT GUIDE

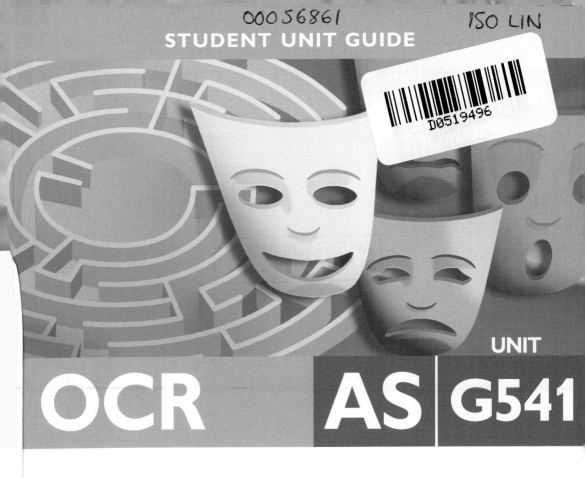

OCR

AS | UNIT G541

Psychology

Psychological Investigations

Fiona Lintern

Series Editor: David Clarke

Philip Allan Updates, an imprint of Hodder Education, An Hachette UK Company,
Market Place, Deddington, Oxfordshire OX15 0SE

Orders

Bookpoint Ltd, 130 Milton Park, Abingdon, Oxfordshire OX14 4SB
tel: 01235 827720
fax: 01235 400454
e-mail: uk.orders@bookpoint.co.uk

Lines are open 9.00 a.m.–5.00 p.m., Monday to Saturday, with a 24-hour message
answering service. You can also order through the Philip Allan Updates website:
www.philipallan.co.uk

© Philip Allan Updates 2008

ISBN 978-0-340-95027-2

First printed 2008

Impression number 5 4 3
Year 2013 2012 2011 2010 2009

Typeset by Phoenix Photosetting, Chatham, Kent
Printed by MPG Books, Bodmin

Hachette UK's policy is to use papers that are natural, renewable and recyclable
products and made from wood grown in sustainable forests. The logging and
manufacturing processes are expected to conform to the environmental regulations
of the country of origin.

Contents

Introduction

■ ■ ■

Content Guidance

■ ■ ■

Questions & Answers

Introduction

About this guide

This book is a guide to the new OCR AS Psychology specification (aggregation code H168), which examines the content of **Unit G541: Psychological Investigations**. It is intended as a revision aid rather than as a textbook. Its purpose is to summarise the content, to explain how the content will be assessed, to look at the type of questions to expect and to consider specimen answers.

There are three sections:

- **Introduction**. This outlines the specification requirements for Unit G541 and suggests appropriate data-collecting activities that will help your examination preparation. It also includes guidance on what to study and how you can organise your studies, as well as revision tips.
- **Content Guidance**. This takes you through the material that you need to cover for the examination. There are sub-sections on the different methods with which you need to be familiar, along with advice on writing hypotheses and operationalising variables. This is followed by guidance on the different tasks that might be set on the examination: evaluating research, dealing with data and designing research.
- **Questions & Answers**. The final section of the book provides sample questions and answers that are followed by examiner's comments and marks. Look at the responses and comments of the examiner and try to apply the best techniques to your own answers.

Getting started

You will need a file (or folder) and some dividers. As there are four methodological techniques, divide your folder into four sections. You should also include a section into which you can put all your assessed work (do not throw it away — keep it and revise from it, rewriting any answers that did not get full marks).

The specification

Unit G541 examines your knowledge and understanding of research methods. Although you are not tested on research activities that you have conducted, it is advisable to carry out as much practical research as you can. This will not only allow you to become familiar with each of the data-collecting techniques, but will also give you first-hand experience of many of the evaluative issues that this book covers.

You should be familiar with the following techniques for collecting/analysing data:
- self-report
- experiment
- observation
- correlation

There will be three sections in the examination, and you may be asked to respond to different kinds of source materials. These include an outline of a piece of research, the data produced by a piece of research and an outline of a *proposed* piece of research.

Outline of a piece of research

You could be given a brief outline of a piece of research and asked to do some of the following:
- identify strengths and weaknesses of the research method in general
- identify strengths and weaknesses of the specific research described in the source material
- suggest improvements to the research and their likely effects
- consider issues such as the reliability and validity of measurements
- consider ethical issues raised by the source material

Data produced by a piece of research

You could be given a table or graph displaying the results of a research and asked to do some of the following:
- suggest appropriate descriptive statistics/graphical representations of the data (you will not be asked any questions relating to inferential statistics)
- draw conclusions from data/graphs
- sketch summary tables/graphs

Outline of a proposed piece of research

You could be given a research idea and then asked to do some of the following:
- suggest appropriate hypotheses
- suggest how variables might be operationalised/measured
- suggest appropriate samples/sampling methods
- outline possible procedures
- evaluate the suggestions that you have made

The examination will not necessarily require you to do all of these tasks and you may be asked combinations of the tasks above. For example, there might be a section that first asks you to comment on the data given and then asks you to suggest alternative ways of measuring the dependent variable. However, this book will cover everything that you might be asked to do.

Conducting your own research

Although it is not a requirement of this unit that you conduct research, it is much easier to understand the principles of good research design if you have tried it yourself. So, if possible, try to collect data using the four techniques required for the examination. The ideas outlined below will help you.

Self-report

This can be any data-collecting activity that involves questioning people directly. It could be a survey of attitudes to something, or a questionnaire asking people about themselves or some aspect of their behaviour. Plan your questions carefully and try them out on a small group of people before you ask your participants to make sure that everyone understands the questions in the same way. This is called a 'pilot study'. Make sure that you avoid any questions that might embarrass or offend people.

Ideas for questionnaires
- ask students about their study habits
- ask students about their sleep habits
- ask students (or teachers) about daily hassles (minor stress)
- measure attitudes to TV violence
- measure attitudes to crime and punishment
- find out how helpful people might be in different circumstances

Experiment

Experiments will be examined in more detail in the Content Guidance section. For now, simply remember that to conduct an experiment you need to collect data in two conditions. This means that you have an **independent variable**, which differs between the two conditions, and a **dependent variable**, which is measured in both conditions. The independent variable could be experimentally manipulated (such as noisy and quiet conditions) or could be naturally occurring (such as maths students compared to art students on a particular task). You should keep the conditions relatively simple. Avoid the temptation to have more than two conditions, as this can get extremely complicated.

If you have different people in each condition of your investigation, this is described as an **independent measures design**.

Suggestions for independent measures design experiments
- Do people have better memory (or attention or reaction time) in quiet or noisy conditions?

- How does the use of different words in questions affect memory (e.g. you could see how verbs such as 'hit' or 'smashed' affect estimates of reaction time, or how words such as 'group' or 'crowd' affect estimates of the number of people)?
- Are words paired with visual images of these words remembered better than words alone?
- How do small changes in information (name, age, description) affect the impression formed of that person?

If you test the same people twice (i.e. once under each condition), this is called a **repeated measures design**.

Suggestions for repeated measures design tests
- a reaction-time test, with and without an audience
- a memory test, comparing people's memory in the morning and the afternoon
- an eyewitness-testimony test, comparing people's memory straight after witnessing an event and a day or a week later
- test to see how many press-ups someone completes alone and then in competition with someone else

Note that some of the above suggestions could be conducted as either independent measures or repeated measures designs. You would need to think about the advantages and disadvantages of using each design (this is discussed in more detail in the Content Guidance).

Observation

This activity involves the design of a coding scheme (or set of categories) to record a particular behaviour. The behaviour can be anything at all, but do not forget that there are ethical guidelines restricting where it is acceptable to observe people without their consent. Try to keep your coding scheme relatively simple — it is not necessary to have more than four or five categories, and you may have even fewer than that.

Suggestions for observations
- animal behaviour (many zoos/wildlife parks have information on primate behaviour, which might allow you to develop a coding scheme to observe such behaviours as mother–infant interaction, time use, grooming and facial expressions)
- superstitious behaviour — do more people walk around a ladder or under it?

- what people do with their litter
- how male and female students spend their 'free time' in college/school
- how people display aggressive behaviour on the sports field
- the use of mobile phones by gender and age

Correlation

Correlation is more a method of data analysis than it is a research method. To conduct a correlation, you simply need to measure two variables that you think might be related in some way.

If you think that two variables will increase in line with each other (such as how much football someone watched on TV and their score in a football general knowledge quiz), this is predicting a **positive correlation**. If you think that the variables will move in opposite directions (such as how many hours of sleep someone has had and how long it takes him or her to complete a task), you are predicting a **negative correlation**.

You can use a variety of techniques to measure the variables, such as self-reports and observations, as well as tests of ability. Note that all you are predicting is a *relationship* — not that a change in one variable *causes* a change in the other. In a correlation, you are not manipulating anything and cannot draw conclusions about cause and effect. You would need to conduct an experiment (where one variable is manipulated and its effect on another variable is measured) to reach this kind of conclusion.

Suggestions for correlation activities
- Is there a relationship between the number of hours of sleep someone has had and his or her performance on a reaction-time task?
- Is there a relationship between regular viewing of soap operas and score on a memory task based on watching one episode?
- Is there a relationship between a personality measure (such as extroversion) and another variable (such as how many times an individual goes out each week, or how long he or she spends on the phone each week)?
- Is there a relationship between a person's estimate of how good his or her memory is and the score that he or she achieves on a memory test?

Data-collecting activities that would not be acceptable

All psychological research needs to conform to the Code of Ethics and Conduct produced by the British Psychological Society in 2006. Many textbooks still refer to this set of guidelines, but there is a new code. Although the 2006 guidelines are still relevant and present in the revised version, the layout of the new code is different and is now based on four ethical principles (see below). You can read the revised Code of Ethics and Conduct by visiting the British Psychological Society's website at **www.bps.org.uk** and typing 'code of conduct' into the search box.

The code is based on four ethical principles:

- respect
- competence
- responsibility
- integrity

The key guidelines for students conducting research or considering the research conducted by others are as follows:

- Participants should give informed consent prior to taking part in psychological research.
- Participants have the right to withdraw from research at any time.
- Participants should be fully debriefed.
- All information held on participants should be confidential.
- Participants should not be placed at risk of short- or long-term harm.

If you are conducting research as part of your preparation for this examination, you should not:

- ask people about aspects of their personal lives, such as involvement in illegal activities, sexuality or other private issues
- use children under 16 as your participants
- conduct any investigation where you are putting people into conditions that might cause them distress or embarrassment
- conduct any investigation where the participants and/or yourself might be at any risk (this might rule out certain kinds of observation or investigation into helping behaviour)
- reveal any confidential information about participants

Skills required for the examination

Three skills, the **assessment objectives** (AOs), are assessed in the examination and are as follows:

- AO1: knowledge and understanding
- AO2: application of knowledge and understanding
- AO3: science in practice

AO1: knowledge and understanding

Candidates should be able to:

a recognise, recall and show understanding of scientific knowledge

b select, organise and communicate relevant information in a variety of forms, including extended prose

AO1 assesses what you know about psychology methodology and whether you understand it. Examination questions here will ask you to identify, define, outline or describe.

AO2: application of knowledge and understanding

Candidates should be able to:

a analyse and evaluate scientific knowledge when presenting arguments and ideas

b apply scientific knowledge to unfamiliar situations, including those related to issues

c assess the validity, reliability and credibility of scientific information

d bring together scientific knowledge from different areas of the subject and apply it

AO2 assesses your evaluation skills, and examination questions will ask you to discuss or suggest alternative designs or methods.

AO3: Science in practice

Candidates should be able to:

a demonstrate ethical, safe and skilful practical techniques, selecting appropriate qualitative and quantitative methods

b make and record reliable and valid observations and measurements with appropriate precision and accuracy

c analyse, interpret, explain and evaluate the results of experimental and investigative activities in a variety of ways

AO3 is the domain for psychological investigations where you do some practical work rather than examine core studies.

For the Psychological Investigations unit, assessment objectives and marks are allocated as follows:

Assessment objective	Number of marks
AO1	10
AO2	10
AO3	40
	Total: 60

Look at the final section of this book for sample questions and answers, and see if you can spot AO1, AO2 and AO3 questions.

Examination guidance

Unit G541 is assessed in a 1-hour examination. Your examination paper will comprise *three* sections — Sections A, B and C. You are required to answer *all* the questions in each section.

Each question is worth *20 marks* and is divided into *three* parts. Some parts will sometimes require short answers, a definition for 2 marks for example, while others, such as a 'describe' and 'evaluate' question part, will require more detail (these questions parts can be worth 10 marks). You therefore need to think about how much you need to write in each answer to guarantee all the marks. One sentence will clearly not be enough for a 10-mark question, but conversely do not waste time writing a whole paragraph for a 'definition' question when a few words suffice.

Whatever you do, do not run out of time. Be strict with yourself. Try testing yourself at home so that you know exactly how much you can write in the time allowed. If you finish ahead of time, reread all your answers and see if you really have written as much and as clearly as you should have done.

Note that there is no distinction between Sections A, B and C in relation to the specification. For example, Section A is not always a self-report and Section B always an experiment. Neither is Section A always about 'outlining a piece of research' and Section B about 'the data produced by a piece of research'. Any aspect of any activity and any part of the specification content can appear in any section.

Checklist of what you need to know

Below is a checklist of everything that you should be able to do. You could tick the points off when you are confident that you can do them.

- [ ] Describe the four techniques (self-report, experiment, observation, correlation). For **self-report**, this should include a knowledge and understanding of rating scales and open and closed questions, and the strengths and weaknesses of each. For **experiment**, this should include a knowledge and understanding of experimental design (independent and repeated measures), and the strengths and weaknesses of each. For **observation**, this should include a knowledge and understanding of participant and structured observation, time sampling and event sampling, and the strengths and weaknesses of each. For **correlation**, this should include a knowledge and understanding of positive and negative correlations, and the interpretation of scatter graphs.

- [ ] Identify the strengths and weaknesses of the four techniques, both in general terms and in relation to source material.

- [ ] Frame hypotheses (null and alternate, one-tailed and two-tailed).

☐ Identify variables (for experiment: identify and explain the difference(s) between independent and dependent variables).

☐ Suggest how variables might be operationalised/measured.

☐ Suggest (in relation to source material) the strengths and weaknesses of measurement and alternative forms of measurement.

☐ Comment on the reliability and validity of measurement.

☐ Describe opportunity sampling, random sampling and self-selected sampling techniques.

☐ Identify strengths and weaknesses of opportunity, random and self-selected sampling techniques.

☐ Identify strengths and weaknesses of sampling techniques described in source material.

☐ Suggest appropriate samples/sampling techniques in relation to source material.

☐ Suggest appropriate procedures in relation to source material.

☐ Identify and describe the difference between qualitative and quantitative data.

☐ Identify strengths and weaknesses of qualitative and quantitative data.

☐ Suggest appropriate descriptive statistics for data in source material (mean, median, mode).

☐ Sketch appropriate summary tables/graphs from data in source material (tables/bar charts/scatter graphs).

☐ Draw conclusions from data/graphs.

☐ Describe ethical issues relating to psychological research with human participants.

☐ Identify ethical issues in source material and suggest ways of dealing with ethical issues.

Links with A2

If you are going on to A2, knowledge of all you will have learned in Unit G541 can be used next year. There are many similarities between the AS and A2 units. For example, the A2 Unit G544 states that 'Candidates should have knowledge and experience of a range of techniques such as experiment, self-report, questionnaire and correlation' — you have already covered these four. It also suggests the design of a specific practical project that you could carry out, for example a repeated measures design for an experiment involving two conditions. Again, you have done this at AS and you know what this terminology means. A2 expands on what you know, so do not throw away your notes.

Content
Guidance

This section looks at the four techniques for collecting/analysing data:

- self-reports
- experiments
- observations
- correlations

Each approach is outlined in turn, along with a consideration of its strengths and weaknesses. Methodological terms and concepts such as hypotheses and sampling are then examined, with suggestions for tasks that you can do to help your understanding. Next, there is a sub-section on answering examination questions, and finally one on the skills that you need to be successful in the examination.

Self-report

Self-report methods are techniques for asking people directly for information. This might be done by conducting interviews or questionnaires. **Questionnaires** may be completed by the participants or may act as a set of questions that the researcher reads to the participant, whose answers are then recorded. **Interviews** may be structured so that every participant receives exactly the same question(s), or may be semi-structured so that the researcher has some standard questions but is able to respond to the participant by asking additional questions or exploring interesting issues that arise from the answers.

There are many different ways that you can ask questions. A simple distinction is between open questions and closed questions. **Open questions** are simply questions that ask the participant to give a response in his or her own words. An example of an open question would be 'What do you think of AS psychology?'

If you asked a number of people this question, you would probably get a variety of types of answers. Some people may simply say that they like it or that they do not like it, while others may give you lots of information. Although asking open questions will give you a fair amount of details, it may be difficult to draw general conclusions from a group of people.

An alternative to this may be to ask **closed questions**, which require the participants to choose from a range of pre-determined answers. An example of a closed question would be 'Do you like AS psychology?' (the choice of answers being 'yes' or 'no' only).

This would not give you as much information about what people actually think about AS psychology, but it would allow you to draw a general conclusion, for example that out of 20 people, 17 said that they liked AS psychology and three said that they did not.

You could get a little more from a closed question by asking it this way:

Tick the statement that best describes your feelings about AS psychology:

1   I like AS psychology a lot.   ☐

2   I like AS psychology a little.   ☐

3   I neither like nor dislike AS psychology.   ☐

4   I dislike AS psychology a little.   ☐

5   I dislike AS psychology a lot.   ☐

This time, you may find that the questioning of the same 20 people produces the following results:
- 6 say that they like AS psychology a lot
- 11 say that they like AS psychology a little
- 1 says that he or she neither likes nor dislikes AS psychology

- 2 say that they dislike AS psychology a little
- 0 say that they dislike AS psychology a lot

This type of questioning provides you with more precise information. However, there may still be problems. For example, do you know that everyone you asked interpreted the phrases 'a little' or 'a lot' in the same way? Maybe someone who said that he or she liked AS psychology a lot actually has the same feelings as someone who said that he or she only liked it a little but has interpreted the words differently. In this case, perhaps the distinction between 'a little' and 'a lot' is too broad and there should be another category in between.

An alternative to this would be to use a **rating scale** (sometimes referred to as a Likert scale). If you used a rating scale to ask the question, it would look like this:

> Using the scale below where 1 = I dislike AS psychology a lot and 10 = I like AS psychology a lot, choose the number that best reflects your feelings about AS psychology:
>
> 1   2   3   4   5   6   7   8   9   10

This would give you an even more detailed set of results. This time, you might have results similar to this:

Ratings of AS Psychology where 1 = dislike a lot and 10 = like a lot	Number of people
1	0
2	1
3	2
4	1
5	1
6	4
7	4
8	2
9	3
10	2

This type of questioning has produced a great deal of information about the participants' feelings about AS psychology. However, you still need to be cautious in interpreting this information. Would everyone interpret the numerical scale in the same way? Do the four people who chose number 6 all have exactly the same opinion about how much they like AS psychology? You should not assume that they do, and so you need to take care when drawing conclusions from these results.

> **Task**
> - Design a questionnaire asking AS psychology students for their opinions of their psychology course. Your questionnaire should ask a range of open and closed questions and contain at least one rating scale. Try to ask more than just how much they like the course.
> - When you have finished your questionnaire, try to evaluate it. Are there any problems with any of the questions? What could you conclude from the results if you used this questionnaire? What would you need to be cautious about?

Strengths and weaknesses of self-reports

Strengths	Weaknesses
• Asking people directly, rather than trying to work out reasons for their behaviour from other methods, such as observation	• People may give answers based on social desirability bias, acquiescence or response set
• Large amounts of data can be collected relatively quickly and cheaply, which can increases representativeness and generalisability	• Questions/scales may be interpreted differently by participants
• Replicable	• Closed questions may force people into choosing answers that do not reflect their true opinion
• Closed questions are easy to score/analyse	• Open questions are extremely difficult to score/analyse

Experiment

Psychologists use experiments to test their ideas. There are several kinds of experiments but they all attempt to measure the effect of one variable on another. Here laboratory experiments, field experiments and natural experiments will be examined.

Laboratory experiments

A laboratory experiment is an experiment conducted in a controlled situation. The researcher will manipulate one variable (the **independent variable** or **IV**) and measure its effect on another variable (the **dependent variable** or **DV**). For example, if you thought that the amount of light in a room affected the amount of work that students did, you could test this experimentally by varying the amount of light that was in the room and measuring the amount of work that was done. There are a number of different experimental designs that could be used to do this.

Independent measures design

An independent measures design is one that uses two (or more) conditions, with different participants in each condition. To use an independent measures design for the 'light and work' experiment mentioned above, you would test one group of participants in a well-lit room and another group in a poorly lit room. You could give the participants the same task to do and then compare how much each group has completed.

Repeated measures design

A repeated measures design is one that uses the same participants in each condition. This time, you would need to test the participants in a well-lit room and then test them again in a poorly lit room. You could then compare the results for each condition.

Task

There are advantages and disadvantages to each of these experimental designs. Try to:
- identify the strengths and weaknesses of using an independent measures design to investigate the effect of the amount of light on the amount of work completed by students
- identify the strengths and weaknesses of using a repeated measures design to investigate the effect of the amount of light on the amount of work completed by students
- decide which design you would use to conduct this experiment and give your reasons

Strengths and weaknesses of experimental designs

Strengths of independent measures	Weaknesses of independent measures
• Participants only have to do the task once so they are less likely to get bored or to work out what it is that is being tested (which may affect how they behave) • The same task can be used with each group	• As there are different participants in each group, there may be differences between them, which means that it is possible that the difference between them is what produced the difference in results (rather than the difference between the two conditions)

Strengths of repeated measures	Weaknesses of repeated measures
• The participants are the same in each group, so it is easier to compare their performance in each condition • You need fewer participants as they will take part in each condition	• Either the participants will do the same task twice, which may lead to boredom or improvement and may help them work out what is being tested, or you will need two different tasks, which may make comparisons more difficult as one task may be easier than the other

There is a third design that can be used that may overcome some of the problems described above.

Matched pairs design

A matched pairs design is one where different participants are used in each condition but the researcher attempts to make the two groups of participants as similar as possible. This could be done by measuring the participants' ability on some appropriate measure beforehand and then pairing those who have a similar level of ability. One of each pair is then allocated to each condition.

Strengths of matched pairs design	Weakness of matched pairs design
• Participants only have to be tested once • Differences between the two groups have been reduced	• A lengthy and time-consuming process that can be quite 'wasteful' of participants as a large number of people would need to be tested to find appropriate pairs

Strengths and weaknesses of laboratory experiments

Strengths	Weaknesses
• Manipulation of independent variables can indicate cause-and-effect relationships • Increased control and accurate measurement • Standardised procedures mean that replication is possible	• Artificial conditions may produce unnatural behaviour, which means that the research lacks ecological validity • Results may be biased by sampling, demand characteristics and/or experimenter bias • Total control over all variables is never possible • There may be ethical problems of deception etc.

Field experiments

Field experiments are carried out in a natural environment, but the independent variable is still manipulated by the experimenter.

Strengths of field experiments	Weaknesses of field experiments
• Greater ecological validity because surroundings are natural • Less likelihood of demand characteristics (if people are unaware of the research taking place)	• Difficulties in controlling the situation, therefore more possibility of bias from extraneous variables • Difficult to replicate • Time-consuming • Ethical problems of consent, deception, invasion of privacy etc.

Natural experiments

Natural experiments take place in circumstances that allow the researcher to examine the effect of a naturally occurring independent variable. Natural experiments are often used where artificial manipulation of a variable would be impossible or unethical. For example, it is not possible to manipulate artificially age or sex for experimental reasons, so an experiment comparing different age groups or comparing the performance of males and females would be a natural experiment.

Strengths of natural experiments	Weaknesses of natural experiments
• Greater ecological validity since the change in the independent variable is a natural one • Allows researchers to investigate areas that would otherwise be unavailable to them • Increased validity of findings due to lack of experimenter manipulation • If subjects are unaware of being studied, there will be little bias from demand characteristics	• Difficult to infer cause and effect due to lack of control over extraneous variables and no manipulation of independent variable • Impossible to replicate exactly • May be subject to bias if participants know that they are being studied • Ethical problems of consent, deception, invasion of privacy etc.

Observation

In an observation, the researcher will simply observe without manipulation and attempt to record the behaviour that he or she observes. The fact that there is no manipulation makes this a non-experimental technique. Although this can be done by simply trying to write down everything that is observed, it is more usual to develop a coding scheme or set of categories that can simply be ticked when the appropriate behaviours are seen.

Observations can be carried out using the following techniques:
- **Time sampling**, where the researcher observes everything that occurs within a certain time period. For example, recording behaviour in a classroom could be done by observing each child for 1 minute and recording what he or she is doing, then moving on to the next child. Recording mother–infant interactions could be done by coding the behaviour at 30-second intervals.
- **Event sampling**, where the researcher records a specific event every time it occurs. For example, recording behaviour in a classroom could be done by producing a list of all possible behaviours (perhaps by conducting a pilot study) and then ticking the appropriate box every time the behaviour is observed.

Observations can be conducted within laboratory settings (**controlled observation**) or in more natural environments (**naturalistic observations**). A further possibility is to conduct participant observation where the researcher becomes a part of the group that is being observed.

> **Task**
> You have been asked to conduct an observation to find out exactly what sixth form students use their study room for. Suggest the categories that you could use for this observation, then outline some of the problems that you might encounter if you were to conduct this observation.

If observations are conducted by more than one observer, it is important to consider the issue of **inter-rater reliability**. This is the extent to which observers agree on the way that behaviours should be categorised. High inter-rater reliability means that the observers are in close agreement. High levels of inter-rate reliability can be achieved through training observers and making categories clear and unambiguous.

Strengths and weaknesses of observations

Strengths	Weaknesses
• High ecological validity where 'real' behaviour is being observed — especially where people are unaware of being observed • Can produce extremely 'rich' data • Low demand characteristics where people are unaware of being observed • Can be used where it would be difficult or unethical to manipulate variables • Can be used to generate hypotheses for further experimental research	• Lack of control over variables as nothing is being manipulated/held constant • Difficult to conclude cause-and-effect relationships as no variables are being manipulated • Can be subject to observer bias • Can be difficult to ensure inter-rater reliability • Extremely difficult to replicate • Ethical issues if people are observed without their permission • Problems of demand characteristics if people are observed with their permission

Note that observation can also be used as a technique for collecting data within an experiment. For example, in a study of the effects of observing television violence, children might be exposed to different degrees of violence (keeping ethical considerations in mind of course), then their levels of aggression could be measured using an observation. This would still be an experiment.

Correlation

Strictly speaking, correlation is a method of statistical analysis rather than a research method. A correlation shows a relationship between two variables. No manipulation takes place and both variables are measured. Results are generally plotted on a scatter graph that displays the direction and strength of the relationship.

A positive correlation between two variables means that as the scores on one variable increase, so do the scores on the other variable (see Figure 1). However, this does not mean that the increase in one variable *causes* the increase on the other variable; it simply means that the two variables are positively related.

A negative correlation between two variables means that as the scores on one variable increase, the scores on the other variable decrease (see Figure 2). Again, this does not show cause and effect, but simply that the variables are negatively related.

Imagine that a teacher decided to find out the relationship between the number of hours of sleep that a student had on the previous night and the speed at which he or she can work. This is not an experiment, so the teacher does not need to manipulate

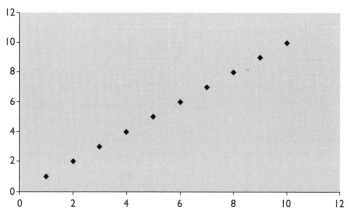

Figure 1 A perfect positive correlation

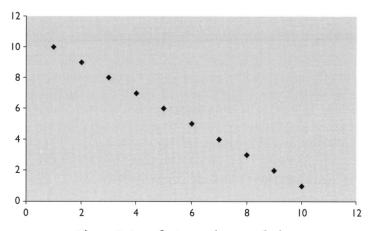

Figure 2 A perfect negative correlation

anything. She would just need to decide how to measure each of these variables, and this means using whatever techniques she felt were most appropriate.

To measure the number of hours of sleep that a student has had the previous night, a self-report technique could be used and the student could simply be asked to give the information, for example in answer to the following question: 'How many hours of sleep did you get last night?'

This looks like a straightforward question and is certainly a simple technique for getting the data. However, it might be that the participants do not actually know the answer to this question and they may simply guess. It might also be that they think the teacher is asking them because of an ulterior motive, so they may say that they had 8 hours of sleep in order to avoid being told off for not getting enough sleep on a school night. They may also say that they only had 3 hours of sleep because they are being asked in front of the rest of the class and they think that this answer would impress their friends.

This shows that correlation may be affected by the strengths and weaknesses associated with the choice of measurement.

> **Task 1**
> The teacher decides to use the speed at which students can complete a jigsaw puzzle as her measure of 'speed of work'. Suggest what strengths and weaknesses this choice of measurement might have, then propose two other ways in which 'speed of work' might be measured.

So what can we conclude from this research? Suppose that the teacher finds that the students who had the most sleep completed the jigsaw the fastest. This does not mean that she can infer that getting a good night's sleep causes an improvement in the speed of work. All she has shown is that there is a relationship between the two variables. There may be a third variable that explains this relationship (such as dedicated students working harder and not going out late as much), or the relationship may simply be coincidence. However, the results of this correlation could be used to generate ideas for further experimental research that might demonstrate that participants who were allowed 8 hours of sleep completed a task faster than participants who were only allowed 5 hours of sleep.

Strengths and weaknesses of correlation

Strengths	Weaknesses
• Gives precise information on the degree of relationship between variables	• No cause and effect can be inferred
• No manipulation is required, so correlation can be used in situations where experimentation would be impossible or unethical	• Technique is subject to any problems associated with the method used to collect data (e.g. self-report or observation may have been used to measure variables)
• In some cases, strong significant correlations can suggest ideas for experimental studies to determine cause-and-effect relationships	

> **Task 2**
> • Using the correlational technique, suggest how you might investigate the relationship between the amount of coffee that people drink and their stress levels. Explain clearly how you would measure each variable.

- Assuming that you found a positive relationship between coffee intake and stress (as coffee intake increases, so do stress levels), does this mean that you have demonstrated that:
  a drinking coffee makes people stressed?
  b high stress levels make people drink more coffee?
  c neither a nor b
  Explain your answer.

Task 3

Suggest which method would be the most appropriate for investigating the topics listed below. If you can think of more than one method that could be used, consider issues such as ethics, ecological validity, demand characteristics etc. to decide which you think would be most appropriate.

- study habits of sixth formers
- sleep habits of university students
- superstitious behaviour
- the effects of television violence on behaviour
- the effects of noise on memory
- the effect of audiences on sport performance
- attitudes to homeless people
- the relationship between time spent watching television and time spent doing homework
- mobile phone usage
- aggressive behaviour in the playground

Methodological terms and concepts

Hypotheses

A hypothesis is a testable statement. It establishes what you think the relationship between two variables is.

For an experiment, the **alternate hypothesis** (sometimes called the experimental hypothesis) would state how one variable (the independent variable, or IV) is likely to affect another variable (the dependent variable, or DV). If you are asked to write a hypothesis in the examination, you need to think carefully about the appropriate wording.

The following are examples of clearly worded hypotheses:
- Participants will remember more words from a list of 20 nouns when learning takes place in a quiet environment than when learning takes place in a noisy environment.
- Participants will complete more press-ups in 2 minutes when in competition with another person than when alone.

These are clear statements: we know exactly what each variable is and how the independent variable will affect the dependent variable. These are also **one-tailed hypotheses**, which means that the direction of the effect has been predicted: the researchers have predicted that people will remember *more* words and complete *more* press-ups.

It is not essential to predict the direction of the effect. If you conducted an experiment where you were unable to decide how you thought the independent variable might affect the dependent variable, you would produce a **two-tailed hypothesis**. This would be worded as follows:
- The noise level in a room will affect how many words people remember from a list of 20 nouns.
- Competition will affect the number of press-ups that a person can complete in 2 minutes.

You could also be asked to write a **null hypothesis**. This is the 'no effect' hypothesis and is the other possible outcome to your research: either the independent variable will affect the dependent variable in the way that you predict, or it will not. Conducting statistical analysis on your data would allow you to decide which of these statements is accepted and which is rejected. However, note that you will not be asked to do any statistical analysis in this examination.

Null hypotheses would be worded as follows:
- The noise level in a room will not affect how many words people remember from a list of 20 nouns **OR** There will be no difference in the number of words participants remember from a list of 20 nouns when learning takes place in a quiet environment compared to a noisy environment.
- Competition will not affect the number of press-ups that a person can complete in 2 minutes **OR** There will be no difference in the number of press-ups participants can complete in 2 minutes when in competition with another person compared to alone.

Remember that a null hypothesis is not the opposite of the alternate hypothesis. It is not correct to predict 'more words' or 'more press-ups' in the experimental hypothesis and then to change this to 'fewer words' or 'fewer press-ups' in the null hypothesis — this is still predicting that the independent variable is going to have an effect on the dependent variable. The null hypothesis must predict no effect.

If the research is correlational rather than experimental, both hypotheses need to be worded appropriately. Rather than predicting an *effect*, you are now predicting a

content guidance

relationship. An alternate hypothesis for a correlation might be 'There will be a positive relationship between the number of hours of sleep a participant has had and his or her score on a word-search task'. The null would be 'There will be no relationship between the number of hours of sleep a participant has had and his or her score on a word-search task'.

Task 1
For each of the following hypotheses, decide whether it is alternate or null:
- There will be no difference in the time taken to complete a jigsaw in the morning and in the evening.
- People will complete a jigsaw puzzle faster after drinking coffee than after drinking a non-caffeinated drink.
- There is no difference between the memory scores of males and females.
- Age will not affect performance on a mathematics test.
- There will be a positive relationship between age and ability to solve anagrams.
- There will be a negative relationship between age and ability to solve anagrams.

Task 2
Identify the IV and the DV in each of the following hypotheses:
- Age will not affect performance on a mathematics test.
- People will complete more press-ups in 2 minutes when in competition than when working alone.
- Males will complete a football-related word search faster than females.
- Eating breakfast improves performance on a reaction-time task.
- Participants will achieve a higher score on a memory test when working in a warm room than in a quiet room.

Task 3
Write appropriate hypotheses for the following experiments:
- the effect of music on memory
- the effect of age on reaction time
- the effect of time of day on puzzle-solving speed

Task 4
Write appropriate hypotheses for the following correlations:
- the relationship between extraversion and time spent watching television
- the relationship between temperature and aggression
- the relationship between coffee intake and stress

Operationalising and measuring variables

Most research ideas start out by being quite general. For example, you might want to design an experiment looking at some of the factors that influence memory, generating the following ideas (possible independent variables):

- time of day
- hunger
- room temperature
- stress
- motivation
- competition
- presentation of material — font size, colour etc.

Let us look at presentation of material and specifically font size. This is quite a simple way to operationalise a variable. We now know the specific variable that will be manipulated, so we decide to give one group of participants material to learn that has been printed in font size 10 and the other groups the same material in font size 12. We now have the two conditions of our experiment.

It is important that we only vary one aspect of the presentation of material at a time. In this experiment, we have decided to vary the font size. Everything else must be kept constant (**control**): the participants in each group will see the material printed in the same font and the same colour, the only change being to the font size.

If we were to vary more than one feature, we would have difficulties drawing conclusions from our research. For example, if one group had material printed in Times New Roman font size 10 and the other group in Arial font size 12, we would not be able to decide whether it was the font style or the font size that was responsible for any differences in memory.

Now we need to think about the dependent variable. The ways that memory could be measured (possible dependent variables) include:

- recall from word list
- recognition from word list
- test on content of text

If we decide to use the last suggestion, we would need to find an appropriate text to present in different font sizes and then design a series of questions to test the participants' recall of their text. This might give us 'number of facts recalled' as our dependent variable.

We now have an operationalised alternate hypothesis: 'People will recall more facts from a text presented in font size 12 than from one presented in front size 10.'

The null hypothesis would be: 'There will be no difference in the number of facts recalled from a text presented in front size 12 compared to a text presented in font size 10' or 'Font size will have no effect on recall of facts'.

Task 5

How could you operationalise the following? (Think of as many ways as possible for each behaviour.)
- helping behaviour
- aggression
- stress
- attention
- sleep
- naughtiness in children
- superstition
- television viewing habits

Task 6

You have been asked to conduct an experiment to investigate the effect of time of day on learning. Propose three different ways in which this experiment could be conducted. For each suggestion:
- identify the design that you would use
- explain how the IV could be operationalised
- suggest how the DV could be measured

Now consider the strengths and weaknesses of each of your suggestions. Which do you think would be the most valid test of the effect of time of day on learning?

Sampling and sampling methods

One of the crucial issues when conducting psychological research is the choice of participants. The key concepts to consider here are the extent to which your sample of participants is representative of a larger population and the extent to which you are able to generalise your findings to a larger population. These are obviously linked: a representative sample will allow you to generalise more easily than an unrepresentative sample.

The terms '**population**' or '**target population**' are used to describe the whole group of people in whom the researcher is interested. The term '**sample**' refers to the group of people that are selected to take part in the research.

Different sampling methods
Random sample
A random sample is a sample that has been selected in a way that means everyone in the target population has an equal opportunity of being chosen. This is the equivalent to putting the names of everyone in the target population in a hat and drawing

out the number of names that you require. Usually, the selection procedure is done on computer using random number generators. Everyone in the target population is given a number, then a computer programme generates a random selection of numbers and the corresponding people are selected.

Opportunity sample
An opportunity sample is one that is selected by 'opportunity': the researcher simply uses the people that are present at the time that he or she is conducting the research. This is a popular method for student research, although there are obvious weaknesses with the way of selecting a sample.

Self-selected sample
A self-selected sample is one where people volunteer to take part in a research project.

Task 7

Which sampling method has been used in the following studies?

1 A student selected his sample by going to the sixth-form common room and asking the first 20 people he saw to complete a questionnaire.
2 A researcher put the names of everyone in a school in a hat and drew out 50 names.
3 A researcher went to a shopping centre and asked the first 30 people she saw to answer some questions.
4 A researcher put up a poster asking anyone who was interested in taking part in research to come to the psychology department on Monday afternoon.
5 Every address in a town is given a number, then a random number generator is used to generate 100 numbers. The corresponding addresses are selected as the sample.
6 A researcher advertises for participants in a newspaper.

Strengths and weaknesses of sampling methods

Random sampling

Strengths	Weaknesses
• Everyone in the target population has an equal chance of being selected • Sample is (should be!) representative of target population	• More complex and time-consuming than other methods (especially opportunity sampling) • Can be difficult (or even impossible) if the target population is large and the researcher does not have names etc.

Opportunity sampling

Strengths	Weaknesses
• Quick and easy to select the sample as you simply take advantage of the people that are around you when you conduct your research • No need to select people because of predetermined categories or characteristics	• May be biased as unlikely to be representative of a target population

Self-selected sampling

Strengths	Weaknesses
• May be a relatively easy way of achieving a sample • Can target/request participants who may possess the features under investigation	• Unlikely to be representative of a larger population

Task 8
Using issues relating to sample and sampling methods, outline one weakness with each of the following studies:
- A study on attitudes to sixth-form life that selected an opportunity sample from the sixth-form study room during lunchtime.
- An experiment looking at the effect of noise on the time it takes to learn a poem. The group learning in a noisy room is all maths students, while the group learning in a quiet room is all English literature students.
- A survey of helping behaviour where all the respondents are volunteers.

Answering the examination questions

You are likely to be set three different kinds of tasks in the examination:
- evaluating research
- dealing with data
- designing research

Evaluating research

A typical examination question will provide you with a short piece of 'source material'. This will outline a study that has been conducted and will be followed by a series of questions asking you to evaluate it. The research could be a self-report, an experiment, an observation or a correlation. You could be asked about strengths and weaknesses, alternative ways of measuring the dependent variable, problems with the way that the research has been conducted and ways of overcoming these problems. You might also be asked to consider the effect of these suggestions on the results of the research.

The strengths and weaknesses of each type of research method and experimental design have already been examined, along with those of the different sampling methods. Now we need to look at some evaluation issues, which are crucial when considering research.

Reliability

Reliability means consistency. In experimental research, this refers to the ability to replicate a piece of research. Assuming that a study is replicated exactly, we would expect to achieve very similar results. This is why it is so important that researchers publish details of their procedures: other psychologists can see exactly what they have done and may attempt to replicate their findings.

Reliability can also mean consistency of measurements. In the examination, you are most likely to meet this issue when considering observational research. If an observation has high inter-rater reliability, this means that two or more observers are agreed on how behaviours should be categorised. In other words, it does not matter who conducts the observation since all the observers would record the same information. You can improve the inter-rater reliability by making the categories as clear and unambiguous as possible and by training those observing to use the coding scheme that you have designed specifically for this observation. You can also conduct pilot studies to test out the coding scheme to see if it accounts for all the behaviours that you are likely to see and to identify any problems that might arise.

Validity

Validity means accuracy. A measure is valid if it is testing what we want it to test. It is possible to evaluate the validity of a measurement as well as that of a procedure in general. You may well be asked to suggest improvements or alternatives to forms of measurement in the exam and then to consider their effects. Think in terms of accuracy: will your improvement lead to a more accurate result? Why? For example, in a questionnaire, were the questions worded clearly enough, or might people have interpreted them as meaning something else? This would lower the validity.

You will not be asked about ways of measuring validity, but these include **split half** (for example, comparing the results from one half of the questionnaire with those from the other half) and **test-retest** (giving the same test to the same people on two occasions and correlating the results).

You might wish to consider the validity of the research in more general terms. This can be subdivided as follows:

- **Internal validity**. In terms of an experiment, did the independent variable really have an effect on the dependent variable, or were there some significant confounding variables that have not been controlled for? In a questionnaire, this might include looking at more general aspects of the procedure: could people see each other's questionnaires or hear each other's responses? Would they respond to demand characteristics or be influenced by social desirability bias?
- **External validity**. Can the results be generalised beyond the specific study that has been conducted? This could be considered in terms of **population validity** (the extent to which it would be appropriate to generalise the findings to a wider group of people) or **ecological validity** (the extent to which the findings of this specific study can be generalised to other settings or situations).

Control

The issue of control has already been covered in the section on experimental design but it is worth mentioning again. If we are conducting experimental research, we attempt to control as many variables as possible so that we can be sure that any changes in the dependent variable are due to the manipulation of the independent variable and not to any other variable. If there are uncontrolled variables (and it is virtually impossible to control for everything), they are referred to as **confounding variables**. For example, if we were to conduct an experiment into the effects of the amount of light on the speed at which participants could complete a task but we conducted the first condition in the morning and the second condition after lunch, we would not be sure if any change in speed was due to the amount of light or the level of hunger.

Bias

Bias can occur in many different ways in psychological research, for example in the way that a question is worded or that an observer categorises behaviour. It is possible that the person conducting the research has an idea of what he or she is hoping to find, and even in the most tightly controlled experimental research, bias might be present, for example in the way that the experimenter communicates with participants. Moreover, giving participants full details of the research before they start, while ethical, can often influence the way that they behave.

Bias can be reduced by piloting questionnaires to ensure that the meaning is clear, training observers in the use of coding schemes, using multiple observers and ensuring that there is a high level of inter-rater reliability, and even by using single-blind or double-blind procedures. A **single-blind procedure** is one where the participants are unaware of the aims of the research (however, while this may reduce bias, it may also produce ethical problems). A **double-blind procedure** is one where a second experimenter is used to gather the data — one who has no knowledge of the aims of the research. This significantly reduces the possibility of the experimenter being able to bias the research.

Demand characteristics

Related to the issue of bias are the expectations of the participants. People do not agree to take part in psychological research and then think no more about it. They try to work out what is going on and what the experimenter might be expecting of them. This can produce several effects: the participants either attempt to please the experimenter and produce the behaviour that they think he or she wants, or they do the exact opposite of that they think he or she expects them to do. This has been referred to as the '**screw you effect**'. There is a third possibility: the participants are concerned that the experimenter is judging them and so they try hard to appear 'normal'.

These issues are important to keep in mind when you are evaluating or designing research. Ask yourself what factors might be influencing the participants in such a way that their behaviour is not that which you would observe if they were unaware of being tested.

Social desirability

Social desirability is a similar issue to demand characteristics and is probably most relevant to self-report methods. For example, if you were asking questions about parents' use of punishment, you would be unlikely to get the truth from everybody as people would be concerned with the way that they are presenting themselves. This might lead them to say that they do not punish their children when in fact they do. Would you tell the truth if your tutor conducted a survey to find out how much time people spent on their homework?

Ethics

Ethical issues are considered in the introduction. However, if you were evaluating a piece of research in terms of ethics, you should consider the following:

- Is there any likelihood of the participants being distressed or embarrassed by the research?
- Are the participants at any risk of short- or long-term harm?
- Have they given their informed consent?
- Are they able to withdraw from the research?

You could also consider the implications of some of the guidelines on the research being conducted. For example, if people know that they are being observed, this might affect the way they behave. However, if we do not tell them that we are observing them, we might be breaking the ethical guidelines. Strictly speaking, it is acceptable to observe people 'in a public place', but 'public place' has never been fully defined. Would you be happy to be observed without your knowledge by a psychologist or a psychology student?

Dealing with data

In the examination, you are likely to encounter some data in the source material. This could be in two forms: either you will be given a table of raw data and asked to sketch an appropriate table or graph summarising the data, or you will be given a summary table or graph and asked to interpret this.

Drawing tables and graphs

A typical examination question might ask you to sketch a summary table of the following results:

Time (in seconds) to complete a jigsaw puzzle

Quiet condition	Noisy condition
20	26
22	26
22	28
24	28
24	30
26	30

Being asked to sketch a summary table means that the examiner does not want to see the raw data. Instead, you could calculate the mean, the median or the mode of these data and present them in a small table. It would also be appropriate to use the totals for each condition, but in the examples below the mean has been used. The means work out as 23 and 28. Now you need to think about the best way to present these figures. What is missing from the table below?

	Condition A	Condition B
Average	23	28

The problem with this table is that it has not been labelled correctly. It is impossible to draw a conclusion from it as you do not know what the unit of the average is: seconds, centimetres, the number of questions answered correctly, the number of mistakes made etc. Neither do you know what the conditions are. You would lose a lot of marks if you drew this in the examination. The table below has complete labels.

Average time (in seconds) taken to complete a puzzle

Quiet room	Noisy room
23	28

In the examination, you might also be asked to sketch a bar chart. The word 'sketch' is used to let you know that you do not have to draw this precisely. There are marks for selecting the appropriate graph and for labelling this correctly, but none for presentation. Again, the means have been used here, but you could use totals instead. What is missing from the bar chart below?

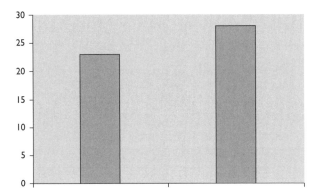

What conclusions can you draw from the graph above? You may think that this graph displays clearly that people completed the task faster in the quiet condition than in the noisy condition, but since it has not been labelled, it is impossible to draw any conclusions from the graph. The numbers could refer to seconds, centimetres, ratings of something or number of words remembered. It is also not clear which condition is which. The graph below has been fully labelled.

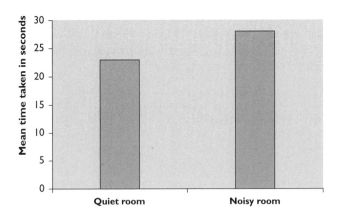

A graph to show the mean amount of time taken to complete a puzzle in a quiet room compared to a noisy room

Here we have a properly labelled graph. Now we can draw a conclusion that on average participants completed a puzzle faster in a quiet room than in a noisy room. This bar chart would be awarded full marks in an examination.

The same basic principle applies for drawing a scatter graph. Remember that you would only draw a scatter graph for a correlation and not for any other investigation. The scatter graph below tells us nothing as we do not know what any of the variables are. You would get a maximum of 1 mark for drawing this.

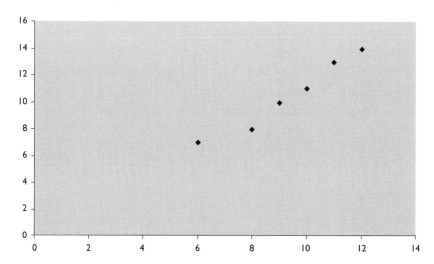

The scatter graph below is much clearer. Now it is possible to draw the conclusion that there is a positive correlation between the estimated score and the actual score on a memory task.

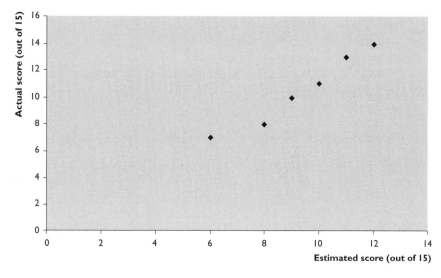

A graph to show the relationship between estimated score
and actual score on a memory test

Designing research

In this section, you will be reminded how to apply everything you know to designing research or to suggesting improvements or alternatives to research.

There are a variety of questions that you might encounter in the examination. For example, you may be asked to suggest:

- improvements to a study and to consider their effects
- alternative ways of measuring variables
- how research could be done using a specific design
- alternative samples/sampling measures and the potential effect on the results

A common question is 'Describe and evaluate a suitable procedure for conducting a piece of research'. This question will usually be worth 10 marks and you will be expected to give details of exactly how you would conduct the research. You may be told whether you are to design a self-report, an experiment, an observation or a correlation, or you may be asked to choose the most appropriate. You have 10 minutes for this question and are advised to spend a minute or two planning your answer before you start writing.

What follows is some guidance on what should be included in an answer to a 'describe and evaluate a suitable procedure' question. Each of the four methods will be considered separately.

Self-report
Describe
- Identify the self-report method that you will use: self-completion questionnaire, verbal-response questionnaire, interview.
- Give some details of the questions that would be included and the way that participants would be asked to respond (open/closed, rating scales etc).
- Describe the sample and sampling method.
- Describe where the research would be conducted and any instructions (time limits etc.) that are given to participants.

Evaluate
- Comment on the strengths and weaknesses of the specific questions.
- Think about the following issues: demand characteristics, social desirability bias, problems of ambiguity of questions and/or differing interpretations of the rating scales, ethical issues. Do not just list these but select the most appropriate and apply them to the research that you have designed.

Experiment
Describe
- Identify the independent variable and the dependent variable in your experiment. Explain how the independent variable will be operationalised.
- Identify the design that you will use and give some detail of the two conditions.
- Explain how the dependent variable will be measured.
- Describe the sample and sampling method that you will use.
- Give details of any controls, time limits etc.
- Include enough detail to allow the examiner to feel that he or she could replicate the research. This might include where the research would be conducted and any instructions that would be given to participants.

Evaluate
- Identify the strengths and weaknesses of the method/design. Do not just list these but select the appropriate ones for the specific piece of research that you are designing and apply them to it.
- Describe any weaknesses in the measurement of the dependent variable.
- Consider the following issues: reliability, validity, ecological validity, sampling methods and ethics, and comment on them.

Observation
Describe
- Describe the categories that you will use for your observation.
- Describe the sample and sampling method that you will use.
- Identify where the observation will take place and details such as where the observer will stand and how long he or she will record for. Will the observation use time sampling or event sampling?

Evaluate
- Identify any problems that might arise with the categories.
- Consider issues such as demand characteristics if people know that they are being observed.
- Comment on the reliability and validity of the measurement. This could include issues surrounding inter-rater reliability and ecological validity.
- Consider any ethical issues.

Correlation
Describe
- Identify the variables in your correlation.
- Describe how each of the variables will be measured.
- Describe the sample and sampling method that you will use.
- Include enough detail to allow the examiner to feel that he or she could replicate the research.

Evaluate
- Identify and explain any strengths and weaknesses in the measurement of each variable. These will vary depending on the measurement that you have chosen, but you could consider ecological validity, reliability and validity of measurements, bias, demand characteristics and ethics. Do not just list these but choose the appropriate ones and apply them to the research that you have designed.

Questions
&
Answers

In this section of the guide, there are ten questions — three on self-reports, three on experiments, two on observations and two on correlations. The sample questions follow the style of the unit and each question is worth 20 marks. You should allow 20 minutes when answering each question, writing as much as you can for the 10-mark question parts and aiming to write approximately four sides of paper altogether.

The section is structured as follows:
- sample questions in the style of the unit
- analysis of each question, explaining what is expected in each part of the question
- example candidate responses — these have been selected to illustrate particular strengths and limitations

Examiner's comments

All candidate responses are followed by examiners' comments. These are preceded by the icon 🄴 and indicate where credit is due. In the weaker answers, they also point out areas for improvement, specific problems and common errors such as poor time management, lack of clarity, weak or non-existent development, irrelevance, misinterpretation of the question and mistaken meanings of terms.

The comments also indicate how each example answer would be marked in an actual exam.

Self-report (I)

A psychology teacher wishes to investigate whether her students are enjoying their AS psychology course. She decides to use a self-report method.

(1) Suggest one open-ended question and one closed question that could be used for this investigation. (4 marks)

(2) Outline one strength and one weakness of using a self-report method for this investigation. (6 marks)

(3) Describe and evaluate how an alternative method could be used for this investigation. (10 marks)

Total: 20 marks

(1) You are asked to suggest two questions and there are 2 marks for each question. The key to getting the marks is clarity. Suggesting a question that is unclear or does not quite match the requirements of the type of question will only get 1 mark. A clear and appropriate example will be awarded 2 marks.

(2) The question asks for a strength and a weakness for this investigation (i.e. students' enjoyment of their AS psychology course). 3 marks are available for each and are awarded as follows: 1 mark for simply identifying a relevant strength or weakness; 2 marks for giving some more explanation, for example why something is a strength or weakness; and 3 marks for an answer that clearly explains the strength or weakness and relates this to the investigation of students' enjoyment of AS psychology.

(3) There are 5 marks for the description and 5 marks for the evaluation. It is important to include relevant details. Just saying 'I would observe instead', will get you no more than 1 mark. Including details about the categories you would use for your observation, where the observation would take place, who would be observed and so on will get you additional marks. For 5 marks, the examiner will need to feel confident that your procedure could be replicated. For the evaluation, simply identifying strengths or weaknesses of the method in general will get you no more than 2 marks. Aim to identify two strengths and two weaknesses of your suggested method, describe them fully and within the context of the investigation of students' enjoyment of their AS psychology course.

■ ■ ■

Candidate A's answer

(1) An open-ended question could be 'What do you like and what don't you like about AS psychology?' A closed question could be 'Do you like psychology? Yes/No.'

   These are appropriate questions and are awarded 2 marks each. (4 marks)

43

question

(2) One strength of using a self-report method is that we are asking people directly rather than trying to interpret their behaviour. One weakness is that people may not tell the truth.

> These are appropriate responses but check the question and the mark allocation. The candidate needs to describe a strength and a weakness for this specific investigation. The strength and weakness identified need to be described in more detail and the answer needs to relate to students' enjoyment of AS psychology. 1 mark is awarded for the strength and 1 mark for the weakness. (2 marks)

(3) An alternative method could be an observation. Observers would need to be trained to use a coding scheme that recorded the behaviour of the students in the classroom. Each student could be coded as follows:
- looks bored
- looks interested but not contributing
- looks interested and contributes when asks
- looks interested and contributes without being asked

This would not be an easy observation to conduct as the observers are being asked to make difficult judgements about the feelings of the students. However, by training them with videos of lessons, they would become better at judging whether the students were bored. It might also be possible to include a rating scale for the observer to rate how interested or bored each student was, although this might lead to problems with inter-rater reliability. Different observers might make different judgements on a scale and so the four categories outlined above might produce the best agreement. You could also video the whole lesson, ensuring that all the students are easily visible on the video so that each individual could be observed throughout the course of the lesson at a later time. This might produce more accurate results than having observers in the classroom trying to make judgements quickly. It would also reduce demand characteristics as the students would not know that they were being observed. However, there might be ethical issues here as a classroom is not really a public place.

> This is a strong answer, but it could have benefited from better planning. Other evaluation points to consider are the problems associated with trying to judge enjoyment through behaviour and, more specifically, whether enjoyment and interest are the same thing. Additionally, is observing just one lesson enough to draw a conclusion about whether a student enjoys a whole course? These points aside, the sophisticated evaluation in this answer puts it near the top of the mark band and the candidate is awarded 8 marks out of 10. (8 marks)

> **Candidate A scores a total of 14 marks out of 20. Most of the lost marks occur on question 2 due to the candidate not reading the question properly.**

Candidate B's answers

(1) 'What do you think of the sixth form?' 'Do you like psychology? Yes/No.'

> The question 'What do you think of the sixth form?' is not necessarily asking about students' enjoyment of their AS psychology course. However, it is not completely irrelevant and is clearly an open-ended question, so it scores 1 mark. The closed question is clear and appropriate and is awarded 2 marks. (3 marks)

(2) The strength of using a self-report method for an investigation into students' enjoyment of A-level psychology is that you are asking them directly. The alternative would be to try to work out whether they enjoyed the classes from observing their behaviour and this might not be reliable. The weakness is that students might not tell the truth if they are asked by a teacher — they might respond to demand characteristics, for example thinking that they need to say yes they do enjoy the subject because they think this is what the teacher wants them to say. Some questions might be problematic because if people are given a choice of possible answers, the one they would have given might not be there and so the results become inaccurate.

> An excellent answer, for full marks. The strength and the weakness are well-explained in the context of this observation. (6 marks)

(3) I would observe the students in the classroom. I would design a coding scheme that included all the possible behaviours that might be seen and then code them. A strength would be that you are observing real behaviour and a weakness would be that students might not behave naturally.

> Candidate B has failed to take notice of the mark allocation. 10 marks are on offer and there are about 10 minutes in which to answer the question. No real information is given about what the candidate would observe. If you are asked to describe a procedure, you need to give details about what would be observed, who would be observed and so on. Simply saying that you would need to design a coding scheme is not enough. The evaluation also needs expanding as the strength and weakness contradict each other. Both are correct, but they depend on whether the students know they are being observed and this needs to be made clear. This answer is only awarded 3 marks. (3 marks)

> **Candidate B scores a total of 12 marks out of 20. The answer to question 2 was excellent, but this was let down by question 3 where the candidate needed to spend more time thinking about the details of the observation that could be conducted.**

Self-report (II)

A researcher conducted a survey to see whether males and females looked for the same things in a partner. He asked them to rate the following characteristics on a scale from 1–10, where 1 is 'not important to me at all' and 10 is 'extremely important'.

- Physical attractiveness
- Intelligence
- Wealth
- Kindness
- Sense of humour

The researcher used an opportunity sample of 20 sixth-form students (10 male and 10 female) from a large city in the UK. The results are shown in the table.

Characteristics	Average rating	
	Males	Females
Physical attractiveness	6.5	5
Intelligence	5	7
Wealth	5.2	5.9
Kindness	6.9	8.5
Sense of humour	4.3	5.8

(1) Outline two conclusions that could be drawn from the table. (4 marks)

(2) Sketch a fully labelled bar chart displaying the results for any one characteristic. (4 marks)

(3) (a) Suggest two problems with the way that this research has been conducted. (4 marks)

(b) Suggest a way of overcoming one of these problems and discuss the effect that this might have on your results. (8 marks)

Total: 20 marks

(1) You are asked for two conclusions and there are 2 marks for each conclusion. A clear and accurate conclusion will be awarded 2 marks. A conclusion that is vague or lacks clarity will only gain 1 mark. A common mistake is for candidates to give an answer such as: 'Females give a higher rating for kindness.' This is incomplete as it is not clear whether females give a higher rating for kindness than they do for some other variable, or whether females give a higher rating for kindness than males do.

(2) You are asked to sketch a fully labelled bar chart for any one characteristic. This means you can choose the characteristic and your bar chart should simply have two bars — one representing the average rating given by males and the other representing the average rating given by females. Just sketching the two bars without any

labels will get you 1 mark. 2 marks will be awarded for an appropriate bar chart with some labelling, and 3 marks will be given for an appropriate bar chart with most of the labelling (or just minor omissions). For 4 marks, the examiner will expect to see clear and appropriate labelling with no omissions.

(3) Part (a) asks for two problems, with 2 marks for each problem. Identifying a problem will be enough for 1 mark, but you will need to give more detail, ideally in the context of the investigation, to be awarded 2 marks. Part (b) asks you to suggest a way of overcoming one of the problems you have identified and to discuss the effect that this might have on your results. There are 4 marks available for the suggestion and 4 marks for the discussion. A brief suggestion will be awarded 1–2 marks and a more detailed suggestion will be awarded 3–4 marks. For 4 marks, your suggestion should be appropriate and clearly described. For the discussion, you need to focus on the effect that *your* suggestion might have on the results. Identifying other effects will achieve no more than 1 mark. An answer that attempts to consider the possible effects of your suggestion will be awarded 2–3 marks, and a clear and detailed answer will be awarded 4 marks. It is possible to discuss one effect in detail or more than one effect in less detail, but for full marks you must make reference to how the suggestion will affect the results.

■ ■ ■

Candidate A's answer

(1) Males think that physical attractiveness is more important. Females think that wealth is slightly more important.

🖉 Candidate A has given two conclusions, but they both lack clarity. The first conclusion should say: 'Males think that physical attractiveness is more important in a partner than females do.' Otherwise, the conclusion given could be saying that males think that physical attractiveness is more important than intelligence. These conclusions are awarded 1 mark each. (2 marks)

(2)

Average ratings for the importance of attractiveness in a partner

🖉 This bar chart gains full marks. The candidate has selected just one characteristic and has produced a clear chart with all the correct labelling. (4 marks)

question

(3) (a) One problem is the scale that has been used. It may be that different people understand different things by the phrases 'not important' and 'extremely important', which means it could be difficult to analyse the results. The other problem is the sample. The researcher has only asked an opportunity sample of 20 sixth-form students, and this sample is not even representative of sixth-form students. The results cannot be generalised any further than the sample that has been used.

🖉 Two appropriate problems have been identified and explained. They could have been explained more clearly, but Candidate A has gone a long way beyond simply identifying the problem, and is awarded 2 marks for each problem. **(4 marks)**

(b) One way of overcoming the sample problem would be to have a much larger sample. This would mean the results would represent the opinions of a much wider group of people and would therefore be reliable and more valid.

🖉 This answer lacks detail. There are 8 marks available here, and candidates should spend around 8 minutes writing an answer. Just saying 'a much larger sample' only achieves 1 mark. The effect on the results is not explained well. A larger sample does not necessarily give you a wider group of people, as the larger sample could still comprise all sixth-form students. The candidate appears to have thrown the words 'reliable' and 'valid' in at the end without any explanation of why the results would be any more reliable or valid. This doesn't add anything to the answer and the discussion only achieves 1 mark. **(2 marks)**

🖉 **Candidate A scores a total of 12 marks out of 20. Explaining the answers in more detail would have resulted in a higher score.**

■ ■ ■

Candidate B's answer

(1) Males rated physical attractiveness as more important in a partner than females did. Females rated wealth as more important in a partner than males did.

🖉 Two clearly stated conclusions, for full marks. **(4 marks)**

(2)

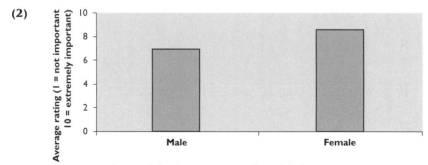

Ratings of the importance of wealth in a partner to males and females

This bar chart gains full marks. The candidate has chosen one characteristic and has produced a fully labelled bar chart. (4 marks)

(3) (a) The sample is too small. It is not possible to draw generalised conclusions about how males and females rate these characteristics when you have asked only 10 males and 10 females. The sample is also all students, which means it is not possible to generalise the results beyond students to a wider population.

Although this answer only discusses problems with the sample, it has identified two different problems. Both have been explained in enough detail for the examiner to award full marks. (4 marks)

(b) This study needs a much larger and a much wider sample. I would suggest a sample of around 200 males and 200 females. This would have to be a stratified sample, representing different age groups, cultures and occupations. It could also include an equal number of people who have long-term partners and those who do not. This would mean the results could be generalised to a much wider population and might give a more accurate picture of the characteristics valued by males and females. This would make the results more useful.

A good suggestion with plenty of detail, which is what the examiner is looking for. The candidate has suggested exactly who would be in the sample and has discussed the effect of using this improved sample, although this could have been done in slightly more detail. This answer is awarded 4 marks for the first part and 3 marks for the second. (7 marks)

Candidate B scores a total of 19 marks out of 20. All the answers are clear and there is evidence that the candidate has read each question carefully and thought about how to answer before writing.

Self-report (III)

You have been asked to design a piece of research to investigate parents' use of physical punishment. You have decided to use a self-report method.

(1) Suggest how you might obtain an appropriate sample of participants for this study. (4 marks)

(2) Outline two ethical issues that you would need to be consider and how you would deal with these. (8 marks)

(3) Outline two methodological problems that you might encounter when conducting this research and suggest what effect these problems might have on the results of this study. (8 marks)

Total: 20 marks

(1) The question asks for a suggestion. There are 4 marks available, so simply identifying a sampling technique will only get you 1 mark. You will be expected to give more detail about where and how the sample might be obtained. You will be awarded 2 marks for identifying a sampling technique and giving some information, such as 'an opportunity sample from a school'. Increasing the amount of detail you give will increase the marks you achieve. For 4 marks, the examiner will be looking for a detailed suggestion about how the sample would be obtained.

(2) There are 2 marks for each issue you outline. Just identifying an ethical issue will get you 1 mark, but giving some detail about the issue (preferably in the context of this investigation) will get you 2 marks. Similarly, identifying a way of dealing with each issue and explaining this in more detail will achieve the full 2 marks.

(3) As with question 2, there are 2 marks for each methodological problem you outline. Identifying a problem will get you 1 mark and expanding on this answer, possibly by explaining why you might encounter this problem, will get you the second mark. The second part could be answered by considering one effect of each of these problems in detail, or by considering more effects in less detail. 1 mark will be given for identifying an effect and a further mark will be given for some elaboration that makes reference to the results.

■ ■ ■

Candidate A's answer

(1) I would use a volunteer sampling method in a school. I would ask the head teacher to send a letter home to all the parents asking them if they would take part. I would try to get 20 parents to complete the questionnaire.

> A volunteer sample is appropriate and the candidate has given some information about how this would be achieved. However, more detail could have been given, for example, would the questionnaires have been sent home with the letters or would people simply have been told what the questions would be about? This answer is awarded 3 marks out of 4. (3 marks)

(2) One ethical issue is informed consent. Participants should always be told what the research is about and should be able to make an informed decision about whether to participate. I would tell them in the letter that they would be asked about their use of physical punishment and then they could decide if they wanted to take part. Another ethical issue is confidentiality. Participants have the right to know that their data are being kept confidential and that no one would be able to identify them from their answers. I would deal with this by telling them in the letter that they could complete the questionnaire at home and would not have to put their name on it. I would also ensure that I did not include questions that asked for any information that could be used to identify the parents or their children.

> Two appropriate ethical issues have been identified and outlined in the context of this investigation. The suggestions for dealing with these issues are also explained well. The candidate receives full marks. (8 marks)

(3) One methodological problem is that parents might lie in response to some of the questions about physical punishment due to social desirability bias. This means they might not want to admit that they smack their children because they might think that this makes them a bad parent. Therefore, the results would not be a true picture of the behaviour of the participants as it would suggest that few if any parents use physical punishment and the results would not be valid. Another problem would be getting a representative sample of parents. Parents who use physical punishment might refuse to take part in the study as they might think they are going to be judged. Therefore, parents who do not use physical punishment might be over-represented in the sample. This would again mean that we are not getting a true picture of what sort of physical punishment is being used by parents and how widespread it is.

> Another good answer that is clear and well-discussed and is awarded full marks. (8 marks)

> **A clear set of answers. Candidate A scores a total of 19 marks out of 20.**

■ ■ ■

Candidate B's answer

(1) Opportunity sampling — this is where you use whoever is around at the time and place you conduct the study.

> Only 1 mark is awarded for this answer. The question asks for a suggestion about how to obtain a sample for this particular study. Identifying 'opportunity sampling' is credited, but there are no further marks for the definition of opportunity sampling given here. (1 mark)

(2) Consent and distress. Everyone would have to give consent to take part and I would not ask any questions that might distress people.

> This is a brief answer, but it does provide some creditworthy material. 1 mark is given for consent and 2 marks for distress and the suggestion to avoid questions

that might cause distress. However, there are 8 marks available here and the candidate needed to provide a much fuller discussion. (3 marks)

(3) Questions could be ambiguous and this might make the results wrong.

Again, there are 8 marks on offer here and the candidate has written 11 words. The first point is true — questions are often ambiguous and this is an important issue when conducting self-reports. However, more detail needs to be given, such as an example or a better description of the effect of asking ambiguous questions. The use of the word 'wrong' in relation to results is also too vague. Lastly, the question asks for two problems, so the candidate has already lost half the marks by only suggesting one. (1 mark)

Candidate B scores a total of 5 marks out of 20. The answers are brief and lacking explanation. There is plenty of time in the examination to provide more detail than this.

Question 4

Experiment (I)

A researcher has conducted an experiment to see if people recall more words from a list of ten words when they learn and recall in a warm room rather than if they learn and recall in a cold room. This was an independent measures design.

The results are shown in the table.

Number of words recalled	
Learn and recall in warm room	Learn and recall in cold room
7	8
7	8
6	8
5	7
4	7
4	6

(1) (a) Suggest an appropriate null hypothesis for this experiment.   (4 marks)
    (b) Identify the independent variable and the dependent variable in this experiment.   (2 marks)
(2) (a) What is meant by an 'independent measures design'?   (2 marks)
    (b) What is meant by a 'repeated measures design'?   (2 marks)
    (c) Outline one strength and one weakness of using an independent measures design for this experiment.   (6 marks)
(3) Sketch an appropriate graph summarising the data.   (4 marks)

Total: 20 marks

(1) In part (a), the examiner will be looking for a correctly worded null hypothesis. There are 4 marks available and you will gain 1 mark for just writing something like 'there will be no difference between the conditions'. If you included one of the variables and wrote something like 'temperature will have no effect on the results', you will get 2 marks. Including both of the variables will get you 3 marks, and if this is all perfectly clear and the wording is appropriate, you will achieve the full 4 marks. In part (b), you will simply be awarded 1 mark for each correct answer.

(2) Parts (a) and (b) have 2 marks each. On questions like these, you will be marked on your clarity. If you have given some relevant information, the examiner will award 1 mark, and if you have given a clear description you will be awarded 2 marks. Part (c) is a common type of question in this examination. You are asked to do two things for 6 marks, so there are 3 marks available for outlining the strength and 3 marks for outlining the weakness. 1 mark will be given for identifying

an appropriate strength and weakness, 2 marks for describing this well and 3 marks for giving this answer in the context of the experiment described in the question. So, if you give a well-described strength and weakness of the independent measures design but don't consider it in relation to the experiment, you will only get a maximum of 4 marks.

(3) The examiner will be looking for correct labelling. If you draw a graph with no labels on the axes or no indication of the units, you will only be awarded 1 mark. The rest of the marks will be given for the labelling. If you have labelled the axes and the scale is clear, you will be awarded the full 4 marks. Remember that it is not possible to interpret a graph if it has no labels.

■ ■ ■

Candidate A's answer

(1) (a) People will remember more words if they learn and recall in a cold room compared to a warm room.

🖉 This is not a null hypothesis because it doesn't state that there is 'no difference' or 'no effect'. This is an experimental or alternate hypothesis as it states that there will be a difference between the two conditions. No marks are awarded. (0 marks)

(b) The warm room and the cold room.

🖉 The warm room and the cold room are the two conditions of the experiment rather than the two different variables. The answer should be that the independent variable is the room temperature (creating the two conditions, warm and cold), and the dependent variable is the number of words recalled. However, Candidate A could have said that the independent variable was the warm or cold room, so this answer is awarded 1 mark. (1 mark)

(2) (a) Different people.

🖉 This just about achieves 1 mark. The answer needs to be explained in more detail. The correct answer is that an independent measures design is one where different people are used in each condition of the experiment and the candidate has not made that clear. (1 mark)

(b) The same people.

🖉 Again, the candidate hints at the correct answer and just manages to achieve 1 mark. The correct answer is that a repeated measures design uses the same people in each condition of the experiment and this has not been clearly explained. (1 mark)

(c) It is better to use different people in each condition so they don't get bored.

🖉 This is a very brief answer for a question worth 6 marks. The candidate needed to outline a specific strength and weakness of the independent measures design for investigating the effect of room temperature on recall. No weakness is mentioned so the candidate has lost those marks. However, although basic and lacking detail, the candidate's answer is correct and is awarded 1 mark. (1 mark)

(3)

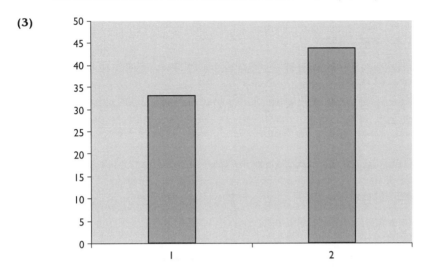

This graph needs labels. Rather than using 1 and 2, the graph should make clear which condition was the warm room and which condition was the cold room. There should also be a label making it clear that the scale 0–50 refers to the total numbers of words recalled by all participants in that condition. As it is not possible to conclude anything from this graph, the candidate is only awarded 1 mark out of 4. Note that it would be appropriate to calculate the mean number of words recalled for the graph, but calculating the total will provide a sufficient summary. Totals may be easier to calculate in examination conditions. (1 mark)

Candidate A scores a total of 5 marks out of 20. This low score is mainly due to the lack of elaboration or explanation in the answers. The candidate may also have read the questions too quickly, which might explain why an alternate hypothesis rather than a null hypothesis was given for question 1 and why no weakness was given for question 2(c).

■ ■ ■

Candidate B's answer

(1)(a) There will be no difference in the number of words recalled when learning and recall takes place in a cold room compared to when learning and recall takes place in a warm room.

   🖉 This is a clearly written null hypothesis that includes both variables and is awarded full marks. (4 marks)

(b) The independent variable is the temperature of the room, warm or cold, and the dependent variable is the number of words recalled (out of 10).

   🖉 This is correct. The independent variable is the variable that is manipulated (the room temperature) and the dependent variable is the variable that is measured (the number of words recalled). The answer gains full marks. (2 marks)

(2)(a) An independent measures design is where different participants are used in each condition of the experiment.

   🖉 Compare this answer to the one given by Candidate A. This is a much clearer answer that suggests complete understanding. Full marks are awarded again. (2 marks)

(b) A repeated measures design is where the same participants are used in each condition of the experiment.

   🖉 As with part (a), the candidate has explained the term fully and achieves the 2 marks available. (2 marks)

(c) One strength of an independent measures design is that participants are less likely to get bored because they only have to do one condition and so may not be able to work out what the experimenter is trying to do. One weakness is that the different groups of participants may differ on some crucial variable. For example, in this experiment, the people in the cold room may have had better memories than the people in the warm room and this might mean that the temperature of the room had nothing to do with the difference in the results. It might have been better to conduct this experiment using a repeated measures design.

   🖉 A strength has been identified and explained to some extent. Rather than just saying that people are less likely to get bored (as Candidate A did), Candidate B has explained that this is because they are only taking part in one condition of the experiment. There is an implied comparison here with a repeated measures design (where participants would take part in both conditions), although this comparison could have been made more explicit. The strength has not been given in the context of the experiment, which is to see how room temperature affects recall, so this part of the answer is only awarded 2 marks out of the 3 available. The weakness has been clearly described and has been given in the context of the experiment, so is awarded the full 3 marks. (5 marks)

(3)

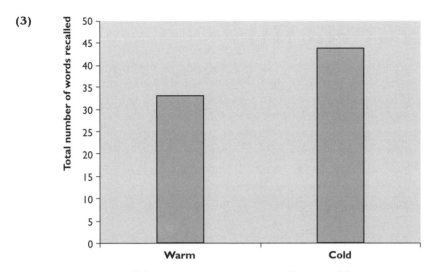

Recall in a warm room compared to a cold room

This is a clear, well-labelled graph. It is apparent what the two conditions are (warm and cold, rather than 1 and 2 or A and B), and the 0–50 scale has been explained. This graph gains full marks. (4 marks)

This is an excellent set of answers that only lose 1 mark out of the possible 20.

5

Experiment (II)

A psychology teacher wishes to see if there is a correlation between her students' liking for psychology and the score they achieve on a classroom test. She asks them to rate their enjoyment of psychology on a 1–10 scale where 1 is 'I don't enjoy psychology at all' and 10 is 'I enjoy psychology more than any other subject I have studied'. She then gave her students a multiple-choice test with 20 questions covering the material they had been studying over the past few weeks. The results are shown in the table.

Participant	Enjoyment of psychology self-rating	Score on a 20 question multiple-choice test
1	10	18
2	10	20
3	8	19
4	8	15
5	8	16
6	7	13
7	5	10
8	5	12
9	4	2
10	1	0

(1) Suggest an appropriate hypothesis for this study. (4 marks)

(2) From the data in the table:
  (a) What is the modal score for enjoyment of psychology? (1 mark)
  (b) What is the median result for the multiple-choice test? (1 mark)
  (c) Sketch a scattergraph of the data given in the table. (4 marks)

(3) (a) Suggest one problem with the measurement of enjoyment and one problem with the measurement of achievement. (4 marks)
  (b) Describe and evaluate an alternative way of measuring one of these variables. (6 marks)

Total: 20 marks

(1) You are asked for an appropriate hypothesis for this study. The study is correlational, so writing a hypothesis for an experiment will not gain you any marks. A hypothesis that says something like 'there will be a correlation between the scores' will be awarded 1 mark. Including both the variables clearly within the hypothesis will gain 2–3 marks. 4 marks will be awarded to a hypothesis that includes all the relevant information and is clearly and appropriately worded.

(2) For parts (a) and (b), there is simply 1 mark for the correct answer. In part (c), if you simply plot the points without scales or labels, you will be awarded 1 mark. A graph with some labelling but significant omissions will be awarded 2 marks, and one with only minor omissions will be awarded 3 marks. A graph that has been fully and clearly labelled will gain the full 4 marks. Remember that you are just being asked to 'sketch' the graph, so there are no marks for accuracy of scale.

(3) Part (a) asks for two problems and there are 2 marks for each problem. The examiner will award 1 mark if you simply identify a problem and another mark if you describe the problem clearly. Part (b) asks you to describe an alternative way of measuring one of the variables and to evaluate this. There will be 3 marks for your description and 3 marks for your evaluation. For the description, simply identifying an alternative (e.g. 'observation') will get you 1 mark, but you will need increasing detail about exactly how you are going to measure the variable to achieve further marks. For 3 marks, it is worth trying to identify and explain (in context) one strength and one weakness of your suggestion. Identifying strengths and weaknesses will get you 1 mark, explaining or discussing them a little more will get you 2 marks and discussing them in the context of this study will get you the third mark.

■ ■ ■

Candidate A's answer

(1) There will be a significant positive correlation between the rating of enjoyment a student gives to A-level psychology and the score they achieve on a multiple-choice psychology test.

✓ A clear correlational hypothesis, for full marks. (4 marks)

(2) (a) The modal score is 8.

✓ This is correct. The modal score is the most popular score. (1 mark)

(b) The median score is 14.

✓ This is also correct. (1 mark)

5

question

(c)

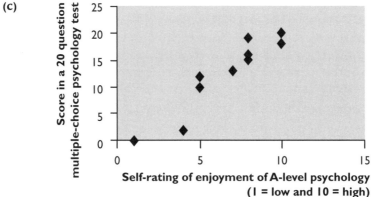

A graph to show the relationship between the self-rating of enjoyment of A-level psychology and a score in a 20 question multiple-choice test

The candidate has labelled the axes clearly and the scattergraph is easy to understand. Full marks. (4 marks)

(3) (a) One problem with the measure of enjoyment is that participants might respond to demand characteristics, especially if the psychology teacher asked them the question. Some students might have felt that they had to say that they liked psychology and some may have exaggerated their lack of enjoyment because they don't like the teacher or are not doing well. Enjoyment is also measured on a scale and different people might respond to the scale differently. One problem with the multiple-choice test is that people might get some answers right just by guessing. If there were four choices for each answer, people might get the right one about 25% of the time, which in a set of 20 questions could make a huge difference. Therefore, this might not be a valid way of measuring achievement.

This is an excellent answer. The candidate has suggested an appropriate problem with both measures and these have been explained well for full marks. (4 marks)

(b) A good alternative for the multiple-choice test might be to give the students a different type of test. This test could be short answers but there would be no multiple choice. It would be less likely that students would get the right answer by chance.

This answer requires more detail. An appropriate alternative has been given — we know that the new test would include short answers and not multiple-choice questions, but we don't know anything else. The evaluation is brief and the answer gains only 3 marks. (3 marks)

Candidate A scores a total of 17 marks out of 20. Giving a more detailed answer for question 3(b) would have increased the marks.

■ ■ ■

Candidate B's answer

(1) Enjoyment will affect test scores.

  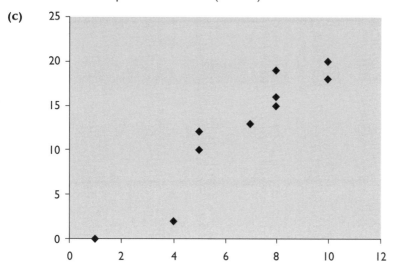 This is not a correlational hypothesis and gains no marks. A correlational hypothesis should state that there is a relationship between the two variables, not that one variable will affect the other. (0 marks)

(a) The mode is 6.6.

  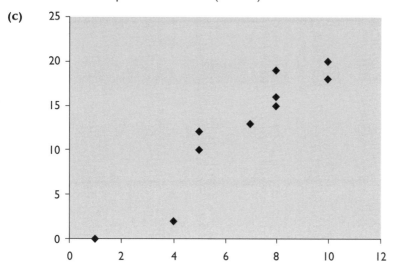 This is incorrect. The figure the candidate has given is the mean rather than the mode. (0 marks)

(b) The median is 13 and 16.

  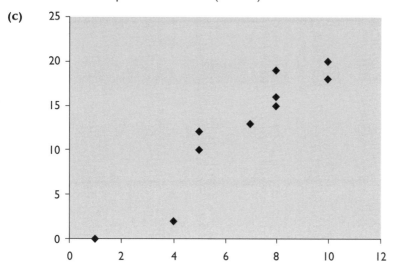 Again, this is incorrect. The median is the mid-point between these two scores (14.5). To calculate a median, you put the scores in rank order and then find the mid-point. If this is between two scores (as it will be in a set of 10), you have to work out the mid-point of those two. (0 marks)

(c)

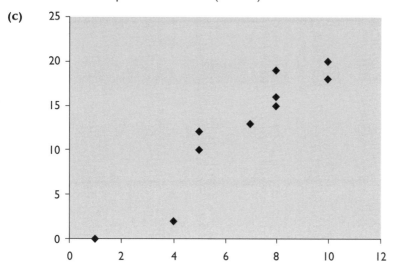

  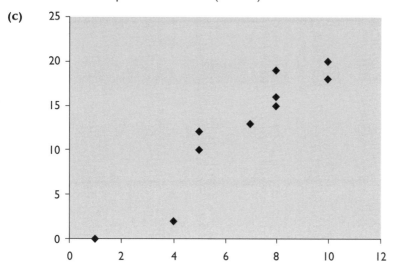 This scattergraph has been plotted correctly but the candidate has not included any labelling. Therefore, the graph doesn't tell us anything and is only awarded 1 mark. (1 mark)

(3) (a) One problem with the measurement of enjoyment is that people might lie. One problem with the multiple-choice test is that people might cheat.

   Only brief answers are given here. The first problem identified is worth 1 mark as this is true, people might lie. However, there needs to be more information explaining why they might lie in this particular investigation. The second point is a weak one. People might cheat in all kinds of tests but are they any more likely to cheat in a multiple-choice test? A generous interpretation accepts this answer as appropriate and 1 mark is awarded. (2 marks)

question

(b) An alternative to the rating of enjoyment might be to ask students to guess how many answers they might get right.

The candidate has not read the question properly. Although this is an interesting suggestion for another variable that could be investigated, it doesn't answer the question set. The question asks for an alternative way of measuring one of the variables rather than an alternative variable that could be measured. This is not an alternative way of measuring enjoyment, so no marks are awarded. (0 marks)

Candidate B scores a total of 3 marks out of 20. More marks could have been achieved if the candidate had provided greater explanation and had checked that the information given was what was asked for in the question.

Experiment (III)

A researcher has conducted an experiment to see if people complete a simple task faster in the morning or the afternoon. The task was a jigsaw puzzle of 100 pieces and the participants attempted the puzzle in a room on their own. The time it took from starting the puzzle to finishing it was recorded. Participants were tested twice, once in the morning and once in the afternoon and a different 100-piece jigsaw was used for the morning and the afternoon test.

(1) Identify the independent and dependent variable in this experiment.　　(2 marks)

(2) (a) Explain why the researcher chose to have the participants attempt
　　　the puzzle in a room on their own.　　(4 marks)

　　(b) Explain why the researcher used a different 100-piece jigsaw for the
　　　morning and the afternoon test.　　(4 marks)

(3) Describe and evaluate how this research could be conducted using an
　independent measures design.　　(10 marks)

Total: 20 marks

(1) The question asks for two types of variable and each correct answer gains 1 mark.

(2) Parts (a) and (b) are asking you to explain why the researcher made certain decisions about how to conduct the research. Both parts have 4 marks, so the examiner will be looking for some detail and explanation. Simply identifying a reason why the researcher might have chosen to conduct the research in this way will get 1–2 marks, but a clear and detailed explanation will be expected for 3–4 marks. For full marks, the examiner will expect to see a well-explained answer that includes the use of appropriate terminology.

(3) This is a 10-mark question with 5 marks available for the description and 5 marks for the evaluation. For the description, the examiner will expect to see a detailed account of how this research might be conducted using independent measures. A brief answer will not achieve many marks. Answers with some detail will be awarded 1–2 marks, increasing detail will gain 3–4 marks, and for 5 marks the examiner will expect enough detail to feel confident about replicating the method you have described. In the second part of the question, you are asked to discuss the potential strengths and weaknesses of using the independent measures design for this investigation. Identifying strengths and weaknesses of this design in general will achieve 1–2 marks. Increasing your focus on the strengths and weaknesses of using this design for this investigation will gain you more marks, and for 5 marks the examiner will expect to see at least one strength and one weakness discussed in relation to the use of the independent measures design for this investigation.

■ ■ ■

question

Candidate A's answer

(1) The independent variable is the time of day and the dependent variable is the time it took them to complete the puzzle.

☑ This is correct, for full marks. (2 marks)

(2)(a) It is probably because they wouldn't be able to copy anyone else.

☑ This is a reasonable suggestion for 1 mark, but the examiner is looking for more as this is a 4-mark question. (1 mark)

(b) So that they didn't remember how to do it.

☑ Again, this is a reasonable suggestion but does not attract full marks. (1 mark)

(3) You would need to have two groups of participants. One group would do the test in the morning and the other group would do the test in the afternoon. This would not be as good as one group might be better at jigsaws than the other and this would be a confounding variable.

☑ Some basic information has been given here and the candidate has offered one evaluative point. The answer gains 2 marks for the description of how to use the independent measures design and 1 mark for the evaluation. (3 marks)

☑ **Candidate A scores a total of 7 marks out of 20. Some more detail would have improved this answer greatly.**

■ ■ ■

Candidate B's answer

(1) The independent variable is the time of day, either morning or afternoon. The dependent variable is the length of time it takes the participant to complete a 100-piece jigsaw.

☑ Correct and worth full marks. (2 marks)

(2)(a) Putting the participants in a room on their own has several advantages. First, they won't be able to see anyone else doing the same puzzle and so they won't be able to copy them. Second, they won't feel in competition with other people or stressed because they can see other people doing the puzzle faster than them. It also means that the conditions are the same for every participant, and this would be harder to control if there were more than one participant in the room.

☑ An excellent answer that scores full marks. (4 marks)

(b) If they had used the same puzzle twice people might complete it faster just because it was the second time that they had done it. They may remember something about doing it the first time that would help them. Alternatively, they may find doing the same puzzle again boring and take longer the second time as they can't be bothered to do the same puzzle twice. Using a different puzzle reduces the first problem (although people might still be better generally when they do a puzzle for the second time) and it reduces the possible boredom created by doing the same puzzle twice. I think the researcher used a different puzzle because there would be less confounding variables than if he or she had used the same one twice.

Another excellent answer. Full marks again. (4 marks)

(3) To use an independent measures design, the researcher would need to obtain two separate groups of participants. One group would attempt the puzzle in the morning and the other group would attempt the puzzle in the afternoon. The researcher would be able to use the same puzzle as the participants would only take part in one condition. The strengths of this design would be that there would be no order effects or boredom effects produced by doing the task twice. Participants would also be less likely to guess the aim of the experiment as they are only taking part in one condition. However, the weaknesses would be that you would need twice as many participants as you would need for a repeated measures design and there might be differences between the groups which would effect the results. For example, one group might include some participants who are very good at puzzles and this group would do better overall regardless of the time of day.

This is a well-structured answer that gains full marks. The candidate has explained exactly how the independent measures design would be implemented and has then offered several strengths and weaknesses of this design. (10 marks)

Candidate B scores a total of 20 out of 20. This competent set of answers shows a good grasp of research methods and a careful reading of the questions.

uestion

Observation (I)

A researcher wishes to conduct an observation of students' food choices in a college canteen and to discover whether boys or girls choose healthier food.

(1) Describe and evaluate a suitable procedure for this observation. (10 marks)

(2) Describe one ethical issue that the researcher needs to consider when conducting this observation and suggest how this could be dealt with. (4 marks)

(3) (a) Explain what is meant by 'inter-rater reliability'. (2 marks)

   (b) Suggest how the researcher could ensure that this observation has inter-rater reliability. (4 marks)

Total: 20 marks

(1) This question is worth 10 marks. Remember that you will have around 10 minutes to answer it. You are asked to describe and evaluate, so there are 5 marks available for the description of an appropriate procedure and 5 marks for evaluation. For the procedure, the examiner will be looking for a fair amount of detail and a clear description. You will get 1–2 marks for giving brief details but not describing a complete procedure, 3–4 marks for increasing detail and 5 marks for a clearly described procedure that the examiner thinks can be replicated. So, you should ask yourself whether you have given enough information for someone else to carry out your observation. This means outlining the categories you would use, where you would conduct your observation, who you would observe and for how long. For the evaluation part, you should try to offer a balance of strengths and weaknesses and relate these to the procedure that you have designed rather than simply offering strengths and weaknesses of observations in general. Again, you will be awarded 1–2 marks for a brief answer that identifies relevant points but doesn't discuss them in any detail, 3–4 marks for an increasingly detailed discussion and 5 marks for a clear evaluation of the procedure you have designed. There is no magic number of points that have to be made, but it is probably worth trying to identify and describe two strengths and two weaknesses and applying these to your procedure.

(2) You are asked to describe an ethical issue and to suggest how this issue will be dealt with. There are 2 marks for each part of the question. Simply identifying an issue will get you 1 mark, but describing it appropriately will get you 2 marks. Similarly, for the second part, if you make a brief or general suggestion, you will be awarded 1 mark, but if you explain your suggestion, you will gain 2 marks.

(3) In part (a), a clear explanation of the term is expected for 2 marks. If your description has some merit but is brief or could be clearer, it will only be awarded 1 mark. Part (b) requires a suggestion given in the context of the observation described in the question. If you simply outline a general suggestion for ensuring inter-rater reliability, you will only get a maximum of 2 marks, as the other 2 marks are awarded for increasing focus on the observation. For example, if you discuss the categories specifically, this would be contextualising your answer, which is what the examiners are looking for.

Candidate A's answer

(1) Before the observation can be done, an observation schedule needs to be constructed. I would list all the food available in the canteen and decide what counted as healthy food and what counted as unhealthy food. I could do this by working out the fat content, for example. Then when I was observing people, I could tick all the food items they bought. This would be better than simply deciding whether they had a healthy lunch or an unhealthy lunch as people may have healthy and unhealthy items on their tray and it would be hard to reach an accurate decision. I would observe for 1 hour at lunchtime every day for 1 week. This would be good because there might be different groups of students in on different days and a whole week should give you a fuller picture. I would observe from a table close to the tills and would have other observers so that no one was missed. There are two tills, so we could observe one each.

> There are some good aspects to this answer. The examiner is looking for two things: details of how the observation would be conducted and some evaluation of the suggestions. Candidate A has given a clear account of what needs to be done before the observation can be carried out and has suggested a good method of distinguishing between healthy and unhealthy food, using the fat content. The candidate has evaluated this suggestion by explaining that it would reduce some of the problems associated with deciding whether someone has chosen a healthy or an unhealthy lunch. The candidate also includes details of the number of observers, where they would observe from and the length and number of observations. This answer is well thought out and, although lacking any mention of gender, it gains full marks. (8 marks)

(2) One ethical issue is consent. In most psychological research it is essential that participants give their fully informed consent before starting the research. However, it is permissible to conduct observational research in a public place without permission from participants. I would not have to ask for permission to conduct this observation as it would be considered a public place and I am not collecting any personal information from the participants, such as their names or any health information. This is an advantage as people would not be tempted to buy a healthier lunch because they knew that they were being observed.

> The issue of consent has been identified and described. The candidate explains how this issue relates to observational research and has linked it to the observation described. This answer achieves full marks despite wandering off the point a little at the end with talk about issues of social desirability. (4 marks)

(3) (a) Inter-rater reliability means that two or more observers record the same information when observing the same behaviours.

> This explanation is exactly right and is awarded full marks. (2 marks)

(b) In this observation, we could ensure that we had inter-rater reliability by compiling the observation sheet in such a way that all the observer has to do is record the food on the tray. The lead researcher would categorise the food as healthy or unhealthy, so there is no room for the observers to have to make this judgement. This is where levels of inter-rater reliability may fall because different observers may judge certain foods differently. We would also need to train the observers to use the observation sheet before they conducted the real observation.

This is a good answer for full marks. The candidate has suggested that the more objective the coding becomes, the more likely it is that two or more observers will agree. So if observers only have to tick exactly what each person buys, there is less room for individual differences of opinion than there might be if the observers had to decide whether someone's lunch was healthy or unhealthy. The candidate also mentions training the observers, which would also reduce differences of interpretation. (4 marks)

Candidate A scores a total of 18 out of 20 marks. Overall a very good answer.

■ ■ ■

Candidate B's answer

(1) I would observe what people bought in the canteen and I would code this as healthy or unhealthy.

Remember there are 10 marks for this question and you have 10 minutes to answer it. Candidate B seems to have spent only about a minute on the question. This answer gives minimal information about the procedure that doesn't go much beyond what is already given in the question. There is no evaluation and only 1 mark is awarded. (1 mark)

(2) I would have to ask for permission from everyone that was going to take part.

The ethical issue has not been identified to begin with and, although the reader can assume that the issue is consent, it has not been clearly explained. The issue of consent is slightly different when considering observational research and it is not always necessary to ask for consent if an observation is in a public place. This answer only gains 1 (generous) mark for a weak attempt at dealing with an unidentified issue. (1 mark)

(3) (a) Inter-rater reliability is how consistent the results are.

This is not quite right and only achieves 1 mark. Inter-rater reliability is how consistently different observers make judgements or record information and is more about measurement than results. (1 mark)

(b) Inter-rater reliability can be measured by correlating the scores from two observers to see how much they agree with each other.

🖉 Yes, this is how inter-rater reliability can be measured, but the question asks for more than this. What if the researcher measured inter-rater reliability and found that it was poor — what would they have to do then? The answer is only awarded 2 marks as it needs to include some suggestion about what to do to ensure that the observers agree with each other. (2 marks)

🖉 **Candidate B scores a total of 5 marks out of 20. The candidate's main problem was spending such a short amount of time on question 1. Remember to check the number of marks available for each question and plan your time accordingly.**

Observation (II)

A researcher has conducted an observation of mobile phone usage. He observed the first 200 people that walked past him in a shopping centre on a weekday lunchtime. He recorded whether they were using a mobile phone and if they were, whether they were talking or texting. His results are shown in the table.

No. of people using mobile phones (out of 200)	33
No. of people not using mobile phones (out of 200)	167
No. of people talking on mobile phones (out of 33)	26
No. of people texting on mobile phones (out of 33)	7

(1) Outline two conclusions that can be drawn from the results. (2 marks)

(2) (a) What kind of sampling method did the researcher use? (2 marks)

(b) Outline one strength and one weakness of using this sampling method for this observation. (6 marks)

(3) Describe and evaluate two changes that could be made to this observation. (10 marks)

Total: 20 marks

(1) You are simply asked for two conclusions, with 1 mark for each.

(2) In part (a), 1 mark will be awarded for an answer that lacks clarity and 2 marks will be given for a clear and accurate answer. In part (b), 3 marks are available for outlining a strength and 3 marks for a weakness. Simply identifying a general strength or weakness would be enough for 1 mark, elaborating on this would get the second mark, and giving an answer which clearly explained the strength or weakness in the context of this observation would achieve 3 marks.

(3) This question asks you to describe and evaluate and there are 5 marks for each part. You will need to describe two changes — just identifying possible changes or giving a brief suggestion would get no more than 2 marks. Further marks will be awarded for increasing detail (the question says 'describe' rather than 'identify' or 'outline'), and 5 marks would be awarded for an answer that described two possible changes clearly. For the evaluation, just identifying a strength or weakness or the possible effects of these changes would get you no more than 2 marks. Discussing these points in more detail and in the context of this observation will be expected for more marks. 5 marks will be awarded for an answer that clearly discusses the implications of the changes on the observation.

■■■

Candidate A's answer

(1) 33 people were using mobile phones. 26 were talking and 7 were texting.

> These are not conclusions and gain no marks. The answer goes no further than repeating the information that has been given in the tables. (0 marks)

(2) (a) An opportunity sample.

> The sampling method is an opportunity sample, but the examiner is expecting a little more for 2 marks. The candidate could have explained why this is an opportunity sample to ensure the second mark. (1 mark)

(b) Opportunity sampling is quick and easy. Not representative.

> The examiner definitely expects more here. The strength and weakness identified are correct and achieve 1 mark each, but both are brief and lack detail. Neither has been given in the context of the specific observation being discussed. (2 marks)

(3) Use more participants and observe in a different place.

> Once again, two valid changes have been identified for 1 mark each, but the answer is brief and vague and the changes have not been evaluated. (2 marks)

> **Candidate A scores a total of 5 marks out of 20. The answers are basically correct, but the candidate has not provided any detail or discussion.**

■ ■ ■

Candidate B's answer

(1) In the shopping centre at lunchtime, only 33 people out of 200 observed were using their phones. This is about 16% of the total and suggests that the majority of people were not using their phones. The second conclusion would be that using a mobile phone for talking is more popular than texting, as nearly four times as many people were talking on phones than texting.

> These are conclusions rather than just results and 1 mark is awarded for each conclusion. (2 marks)

(2) (a) This is an opportunity sample as the researcher simply observed the first 200 people that walked past him at the time and place he was conducting his study.

> This answer gets full marks as it identifies the correct sampling method and explains why it is a sampling method. (2 marks)

(b) Opportunity sampling is quick and easy as the researcher can simply take advantage of the sample that is there at the time they want it. They do not have to go through a lengthy selection procedure. Assuming that the researcher did not want a specific age or other characteristic, the advantages of the sampling method probably outweigh the disadvantages. The disadvantage of an opportunity sampling method is that it does not produce a representative sample as all the people were all in the same place at the same time. For example, in this study this would exclude everyone who was not in the shopping centre and might give a skewed sample in terms of age, gender and occupation.

🖉 This is a clear answer that explains a strength and a weakness and relates them to the observation. Although there could have been more detail, there is enough here for full marks. (6 marks)

(3) I would change the position of the observer. This observation is really looking at people using their mobile phones and walking round the shopping centre at the same time. Maybe more people stop to answer their phones or to make a call or a text. Perhaps observing people in the shopping centre's largest eating area or seating area would allow you to see more people using phones. This would give me a lot more data to analyse. I would also record the gender and approximate age of everyone that was observed so that I could analyse the results in more detail. This would perhaps show that females text more than males, or that older people are less likely to be using their phones than younger people.

🖉 The candidate has given two appropriate changes and explained them. There is some evaluation, but for a 10-mark question the examiner is looking for a little more. Note that the question asks for changes rather then improvements, and this means, for example, that you could identify a strength and a weakness for each of your suggestions. This answer is awarded 4 marks for the suggestions and 3 marks for the evaluation. (7 marks)

🖉 **Candidate B scores a total of 17 marks out of 20. A good answer overall.**

Correlation (I)

A researcher has conducted a correlational study to investigate the relationship between how good people think their memory is, and how well they do on a memory test. The first variable was 'self-rating of memory' and was measured by asking people to rate their memory on a 10-point scale (where 1 is 'very poor' and 10 is 'excellent'). The second variable was 'actual memory' and this was measured by showing them a video of a minor road accident and asking them a series of 10 eyewitness questions.

The results are shown in the table.

Participant number	Memory self-rating	Score on memory test
1	3	5
2	4	6
3	5	4
4	8	8
5	9	7
6	10	9
7	7	6
8	7	8
9	5	6
10	6	7

(1) (a) Sketch an appropriately labelled scattergraph displaying the results. (4 marks)
    (b) Outline one conclusion that can be drawn from these results. (3 marks)
(2) Suggest one problem with the way that 'self-rating of memory' has been measured in this investigation. (3 marks)
(3) Describe and evaluate two other ways in which 'actual memory' might be measured. (10 marks)

Total: 20 marks

(1) Whenever you are asked to sketch a graph or a table, you will be expected to label it fully and appropriately. You will lose marks for any missing labels. So, in part (a), a graph with no labels at all would get a maximum of 1 mark, and a graph with some labelling but most of it missing would get 2 marks. A graph with minor omissions would get 3 marks (e.g. if the axes are labelled but not clearly), and a fully labelled graph would be awarded the full 4 marks. Part (b) asks you to interpret the results. A brief response, one that just described the results, for example saying 'there is a positive correlation', will get I mark. For full marks, the examiner will be looking for a conclusion such as 'the results suggest that there is a positive correlation between...'.

(2) You are asked to suggest a problem. 1 mark will be given for a brief answer with no elaboration or description, 2 marks for an answer with more description and 3 marks for an answer that has been given in the context of this investigation.

(3) 5 marks are available for the description and 5 marks for the evaluation. As with other 10-mark questions, it is important to remember that you have around 10 minutes to spend on this answer, so the examiner is expecting more than a couple of sentences. For the description of the two ways of measuring memory, you will be expected to describe each one fully rather than just saying 'a questionnaire', for example. Your answer will get 1–2 marks if it simply identifies two ways and further marks will be awarded for increasing detail and explanation. For the evaluation, the examiner will expect to see both your suggestions evaluated, so it is worth considering one strength and one weakness for each suggestion. Identifying the strength and weakness will gain 1–2 marks, but further elaboration will be needed for more marks. An answer that gains full marks here will show a good understanding of the terminology.

■ ■ ■

Candidate A's answers

(1)(a) Scattergraph to show the relationship between self-rating of memory and actual scores on a memory test.

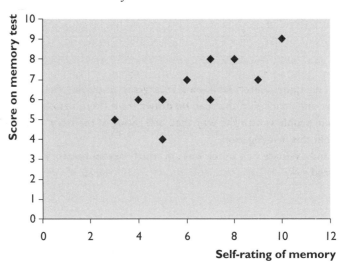

☑ This is a clearly labelled scattergraph and has been correctly drawn for full marks.
(4 marks)

(b) This graph shows that there is a positive relationship between the way that people rate their own memory and the scores that they get in a memory test. As the scores on one variable increase, so do the scores on the other variable.

> *This is a clear answer and gains full marks. The candidate has simply said what the graph shows and has not fallen into the trap of thinking that a relationship between two variables implies that one causes the other. (3 marks)*

(2) Self-rating of memory may be problematic as different people will use a rating scale in different ways. How one person interprets 'poor' may be different from another person, and how one person views a '2' on a 1–10 scale may be different from another person. It is also difficult to assess memory as it is such a broad concept. People might think that they have a good memory for faces or for events but not for information or vice versa. It is also possible that people might respond to demand characteristics in the way they answer this question — either exaggerating or underestimating their own memory ability for whatever reason.

> *This is another good answer worth full marks. (3 marks)*

(3) There are many ways that actual memory might be measured. One might be to give the participants a simple word list. They could be given a list of 20 words and given 90 seconds to learn them. They would then be given another 90 seconds to recall them. The advantages of this kind of measure is that it is simple and large numbers of people can be tested together. The data are easy to analyse. However, this type of measure is not ecologically valid — does a measure of how many random words people can remember really tell us anything about their memory in real-life situations? A second way memory might be tested is to use a recognition test rather than a free recall test. Participants could be shown a number of images (drawings, photos, faces etc.) and then be asked to identify from a larger group those they had seen before. This would also be easy to analyse and may demonstrate something more useful about the way that memory works. We cannot always recall information, but we are often able to identify it.

> *Two good alternatives have been suggested and both have been evaluated. The evaluation for the first suggestion is stronger than the second as it includes a strength and a weakness. Overall, this answer is awarded 9 marks from a possible 10. (9 marks)*

> ***Candidate A scores a total of 19 out of 20 marks. A very good answer indeed.***

question

Candidate B's answer

(1)

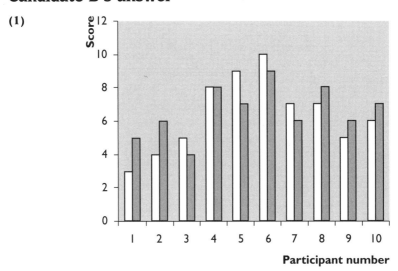

Participant number

🖉 This is not a scattergraph. Candidate B has drawn a bar chart with the two different scores for each person as separate bars. Unfortunately, the chart must have taken a long time to draw, but no marks can be awarded for it. (0 marks)

(2) (a) This shows the scores are quite close together for each person.

🖉 As the candidate did not draw a scattergraph in part (a), he or she cannot be awarded any marks for part (b) because the question explicitly asks for the conclusion to be drawn from the scattergraph. (0 marks)

(b) A 10-point scale might not be enough.

🖉 This is a weak answer and just scores 1 mark. The hint of an answer is there, but the candidate needs to explain in much more detail. (1 mark)

(3) Use Kim's game. Use a video of a crime.

🖉 The candidate can't have read the mark allocation for this question. If a question is worth 10 marks then you should try to spend 10 minutes answering it. The question asked for a description and an evaluation of two other ways in which memory might be measured. The first suggestion to use Kim's game is appropriate, but it needs more detail and an evaluation and is only awarded 1 mark. (Kim's game is where you have a number of objects covered up and you uncover them and give participants 1 minute to try and remember them). The second suggestion is not explained as a way of measuring memory. Although the examiner might be able to assume that the candidate means 'use a video of a crime and then ask participants questions about the video', the candidate has not said this and so is not awarded any marks. (1 mark)

🖉 **Candidate B scores a total of 2 marks out of 20.**

Correlation (II)

A researcher has conducted a study to see if there is a correlation between how stressed people feel and how much coffee they drink. They asked participants to rate their stress levels on a 1–20 scale where 1 is 'not stressed at all' and 20 is 'always very stressed', and they asked them to estimate the average number of cups of coffee that they drank in a typical day. The results are displayed in the scattergraph.

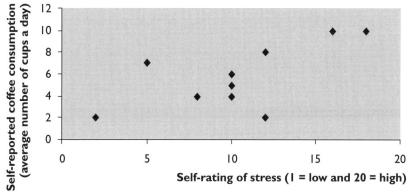

Scattergraph to show the relationship between self-rating of stress and self-reported coffee consumption

(1) Outline two conclusions that can be drawn from this scattergraph. (4 marks)

(2) Outline one strength and one weakness of correlational methods in psychological research. (4 marks)

(3) (a) Outline one problem with the way that stress was measured and suggest how this problem might be overcome. (6 marks)

(b) Outline one other improvement that could be made to this investigation and suggest how this might effect the results. (8 marks)

Total: 22 marks

(1) Two conclusions are asked for, with 2 marks for each conclusion. 1 mark will be awarded for a conclusion that is vague or lacks clarity, and 2 marks will be awarded for a clear and accurate conclusion.

(2) The question asks for a strength and a weakness, with 2 marks for each. You are asked about the correlational method in general terms, so there is no need to relate the answer to the specific correlational study described in the question. 1 mark will be awarded to an answer that simply identifies a strength or weakness but is vague or lacks clarity. 2 marks will be awarded for a clearly described strength or weakness.

(3) In part (a), there are 3 marks available for outlining a problem and 3 marks for a suggestion as to how the problem might be overcome. Vaguely identifying a problem will get no more than 1 mark. 2 marks will be awarded to an answer that describes the problem in more detail, and 3 marks will be awarded for a detailed

description that is clearly focused on the measurement of stress. The suggestion part is again worth 3 marks. For 2–3 marks, you would need to clearly outline a way of overcoming the problem. In part (b), there are 4 marks for each part of the question. For your suggested improvement, 1–2 marks will be awarded for a brief or vague answer, and 3–4 marks for a more detailed response. For 4 marks, the examiner will be looking for a clearly described suggestion. For the second part, it is possible to discuss one effect in detail or more than one effect in less detail, but it is important to make reference to the results of this investigation. Identifying general effects without referring to this investigation would achieve 1–2 marks. 3 marks will be awarded to answers that attempt to address the effect on the results, but may be lacking in detail or clarity. 4 marks will be awarded to answers that explicitly address the effect of the suggested improvement on the results of this investigation.

■ ■ ■

Candidate A's answer

(1) Generally, there seems to be a relationship between the levels of stress and the amount of coffee. As stress levels increase, so does consumption of coffee. We might also conclude that these participants are quite stressed as seven of them rated their stress levels as 10 or higher.

   ✍ Two clear conclusions are given for full marks. (4 marks)

(2) Correlational methods are useful as they allow researchers to investigate variables that cannot be manipulated experimentally. For example, in this research, it would be unethical to manipulate stress levels to see if that affected coffee consumption. However, correlational methods do not tell us anything about cause and effect. They only show that two variables are related in some way. In this study, we are not able to conclude what the relationship is between stress levels and coffee consumption. It might be that stress makes people drink more coffee or it might be that drinking lots of coffee makes people stressed. It might even be that neither of these is true and there is another explanation for the relationship.

   ✍ This detailed answer gets full marks and, in fact, Candidate A has done far more than needed to achieve the 4 marks. Note that the question asks for a strength and a weakness of correlational methods in psychological research rather than in this particular investigation. Although the candidate has used this specific investigation in the answer, it has been used as an example of the strength and weakness given, so is appropriate. Just offering a strength and a weakness of this particular investigation would not achieve any marks. (4 marks)

(3) (a) Stress is a difficult variable to measure. Some people might regard themselves as 'always very stressed' when their stress levels are actually much lower than someone else who might not think that the extreme score of 20 applied to them. Therefore, it would be difficult to know whether self-reports of stress gave the researcher a valid measure. Related to this is the fact that people are only being asked once about their general stress levels — if someone was asked on a day when they were feeling very stressed they might respond differently to being asked on a less stressful day. To overcome this, I would give people a list of the symptoms of stress (such as problems sleeping, feeling anxious, being unable to concentrate etc.) and ask them to rate themselves on these symptoms every day for a month. I would then be able to calculate an average score for each of these symptoms over the period and correlate this with their coffee consumption over the same period.

This is an excellent answer that gains full marks. The candidate has clearly outlined a problem with the measurement of stress and has suggested a detailed solution for overcoming this. (6 marks)

(b) One other improvement I would make to this study would be that I would change the variable 'number of cups of coffee drunk' to 'amount of caffeine consumed'. There is caffeine in cola drinks, tea, chocolate and other things. I would ask participants to keep a diary of their caffeine consumption every day for 1 month and I would give them a list of all the foods and drinks that contained caffeine so they could just mark how many they had had each day. This would affect the results in a positive way as the investigation that has been done has ignored the fact that some people might drink a lot of coke or a lot of tea but not drink coffee. Therefore, this would give us a more accurate picture of the relationship between caffeine intake and stress.

This is an excellent suggestion that has been well-described. The effect on the results has been considered and, although this answer is relatively brief, it achieves full marks. (8 marks)

Candidate A scores a total of 22 out of 22 marks. This detailed set of answers demonstrates that the candidate has thought carefully about each question.

■ ■ ■

Candidate B's answer

(1) Two people drink 10 cups of coffee. Two people drink 2 cups of coffee.

Both these statements are true and both can be seen from the scattergraph. However, they are more like results than conclusions and are only awarded 1 mark each. (2 marks)

(2) Correlational methods are very quick and easy. However, they are not very valid or reliable.

Correlational methods are not really quick or easy and they can be valid and reliable, depending on the measurements that are used. This answer is much too vague and doesn't attract any marks. (0 marks)

question

(3) (a) People might lie about how stressed they are and so I would observe them.

> People might indeed lie about how stressed they are and this gets **1 mark**, but the examiner is looking for more. The candidate should explain why people might lie. The suggestion to observe the participants is appropriate and is awarded **1 mark**, but again, the examiner requires much more detail. Where and what would be observed? **(2 marks)**

(b) I would do this as an experiment. I would give one group of people lots of coffee and ask them how stressed they were, and then I would give another group of people no coffee and ask them how stressed they were.

> The candidate has not read the question properly and doesn't gain any marks for this answer. The question asks for an improvement that could be made to this investigation, not for a completely different study. **(0 marks)**

> **Candidate B scores a total of 4 marks out of 22. The candidate gave only brief answers and failed to read the last question carefully enough to get any marks for it.**